The High Trust

by

Seán Weafer

sean@seanweafer.com

First published 2013

www.hlspublishing.com

ISBN - 978-1482713077

www.SeanWeafer.com
Copyright © Seán Weafer

The moral right of Seán Weafer to be identified as the author of this work has been asserted by him in accordance with the Copyright, Designs and Patents Act 1988.

All rights reserved. No part of this publication may be reproduced, stored or transmitted in any form, or by any means, electronic, mechanical or photocopying, recording or otherwise, without express written permission of the author.

Limit of Liability/Disclaimer of Warranty: This book is designed to provide information about the subject matter. It is sold with the understanding that the publisher and authors are not engaged in rendering legal, coaching or other professional services. While the publisher and author have used their best efforts in preparing this book, they make no representations or warranties with respect to the accuracy or completeness of the contents of this book and specifically disclaim any implied warranties of merchantability or fitness for a particular purpose. No warranty may be created or extended by sales representatives or written sales materials. This book is not intended or should be a substitute for therapy or professional advice. The views and opinions expressed in this page are strictly those of the author. The advice and strategies contained herein may not be suitable for your situation. The publisher is not engaged in rendering professional services, and you should consult a competent professional where appropriate. Neither the publisher nor author shall be liable for any loss of profit or any other commercial damages, including but not limited to special, incidental, consequential, or other damages. This document is provided for educational purposes only. The reader assumes all risk and responsibility for the usage of any information or ideas contained in this guide. If you do not wish to be bound by the above, you may return the book to the publisher for a full refund.

Dedication

To my wife Sharon – for all her compassion, love and courage.

To my sons, Nicholas and Gregory – for being the best boys any dad could wish for.

For my Mom (Eileen), my Dad (Peter) and sisters (Máire, Áine, Eileen, Cliona and Sinead) – for the laughs and the debates we have shared.

Acknowledgements

First, my thanks to my editor Helen Stothard of HLS Business Solutions (UK) without whose expertise in editing, design and publishing this would have taken a lot more time to come to market.

Secondly, to my colleagues and friends in the Professional Speaking Association in the UK, who always serve to encourage, inspire and support – especially my two good friends and colleagues in my speaking mastermind group Lesley Everett and Alan Stevens and to our late friend and all round nice guy Kenny Harris.

Third, to my clients for the opportunity of working with them and to be of service to them.

Lastly to you the reader for taking up this book and choosing to take the first step to becoming a High Trust Adviser™. Enjoy the journey.

Praise for The High Trust Adviser

'In this book Sean provides a powerful new focus on how important social intelligence is in creating and sustaining a high trust relationship - particularly with internal Customers'
Gerard Murnaghan, Sales Director & Head of Commercial Industries, Oracle Europe

'Captures on paper what was quite simply the best and most relevant training I have experienced in 20 years of sales'
Peter Russell, Head of NI Public Sector and Major Accounts, British Telecom

'This is a great book for those who need to build relationships with clients, connect in a way that enhances that relationship and delivers better returns for all parties to it. This book will be useful for even the most experienced professional and will undoubtedly explore areas of immediate improvement'
Nick Cann, Chief Executive, Institute of Financial Planning, UK

'The High Trust Adviser is a practical and really helpful programme, which has enabled my team to achieve better results and to continue to grow and develop their confidence in building powerful relationships. The book brings this programme to life in a fun and insightful way.'
Mary Rose Burke, Director of Pharmacy, Boots Ireland.

The High Trust Adviser by Seán Weafer

'In The High Trust Adviser Sean Weafer clearly guides the individual on how to become an adviser that can meet and exceed a client's needs and sustain a mutually beneficial and lasting business connection. The chapter on intelligence quotient v's social intelligence is food for thought for all professional advisers.'

Liz Hughes Head - ACCA Ireland

'Easy to read, simple and practical advice on how to grow business revenues using low-threat and high-permission techniques. Perfect for professional advisers and business professionals.'

Colin Feely | Partner, Corporate Audit, Grant Thornton

The High Trust Adviser by Seán Weafer

Contents

Dedication 5

Acknowledgements 6

Praise for The High Trust Adviser 7

Introduction 11

Chapter 1: Trust is No Longer Enough 13

Chapter 2: Business Development Expectations 15

Chapter 3: The Co-Factor 16

Chapter 4: IQ v SQ 17

Chapter 5: The Million Dollar Message 25

Chapter 6: How to Get 'Invited to Sell' 34

Chapter 7: Networking Etiquette 49

Chapter 8: First Contact 55

Chapter 9: Selling 'In Colour' 75

Chapter 10: Advanced Questioning & Influencing Skills 90

Chapter 11: Learning to Love Objections 105

Chapter 12: Presenting for Profit 112

Chapter 13: Creating a Success Mindset 125

Chapter 14: Practical Performance Goals 148

Chapter 15: The 6 'C' Success Model 161

Chapter 16: Managing Your Professional Time 167

Chapter 17: Profiting in Challenging Times 175

About Seán Weafer 184

Contact Seán Weafer 187

Discover How to Use the Power of Social Intelligence to Build High Trust and High Profits in Business Today.

Introduction

Just being an expert today is no longer enough. Today, just to get to use our expertise for clients, we must have to be an expert in building 'high trust relationships' so that clients have *absolutely no hesitation* in calling us first when they have a need – instead of the competition.

We have to learn how to use our SQ (social intelligence) so that we can deploy our IQ (technical intelligence) profitably.

In the High Trust Adviser™ book and seminar programme I've distilled what the world's greatest 'rain makers', relationship management and business professionals do naturally, into a proven system of low pressure, high permission business development.

This book is for key account/relationship managers, business professionals, owners and entrepreneurs – rather than just sales people.

Why? Because usually sales people are often just narrowly focused on opening a sale and then hand it to someone else to manage.

But account managers, business owners and professionals must also nurture relationships and through effective and considered service, extend and monetise the 'life time value' of the client - thus creating long-term and sustainable revenue streams for a business.

By 'life time value' I mean the long-term and sustainable revenues that can be earned by providing a continuous level of service and support to a client (and not just a one–off deal).

The world has changed for relationship managers, business advisers and many entrepreneurs. In the past it was enough simply to manage a relationship but now a series of other key factors are impacting on our role.

This book shows you how to become a modern High Trust Adviser™. It takes you step-by-step through various aspects and skills of the role to help you to create and nurture your clients – become more successful, happier and prosperous as a result.

Chapter 1: Trust is No Longer Enough

Today it is not enough just to be trusted by a client or prospect. Now we have to create a 'high trust' relationship.

But just what do I mean by 'high trust'? Have you ever noticed that there are varying levels of trust in relationships and especially in professional relationships?

For example we have relationships with people that we trust – yet we don't share everything with them. We keep certain things to ourselves.

However we also have relationships with people with whom we have a high degree of trust and we share everything with them.

We have absolutely no reservation or hesitation whatsoever in sharing everything with them because we see them as our 'Go To' person if we have a problem that needs solving. We usually call *them* before we call anyone else.

This is what I call a 'high trust' relationship and is the ideal place for us as high trust business advisers or relationship managers.

Today's business advisers and relationship managers have to be able to create personal relationships that prospects and clients find *compelling and engaging* and which encourages them to share all their concerns, wants and needs with us - seeing us as partners in their business rather than merely 'solution providers'. This can create boundless opportunities for us.

Clients always see a 'High Trust Adviser' as *essential* to their business – the 'go to' person whenever they have a need.

Chapter 2: Business Development Expectations

In the past the job of an account manager or business adviser was mostly to serve and maintain existing relationships. Today, however, much more is required of us. Now we are expected to find ways *to create* new relationships and revenue streams.

Whether that is about creating new relationships within existing businesses or whether we have to engage with the wider market place, we are now charged with delivering on new relationships and new revenues.

This demands a different set of skills than were needed before and this book details those critical skills.

An additional element is that unless we are continually developing business contacts many of our existing contacts may quickly be of little value to us – because decision making continues to move up to more senior levels within businesses.

With the increasing need to engage with new contacts this creates the extra challenge of how we get access to these new decision makers and hold their attention in a way that allows us to make an impact.

Chapter 3: The Co-Factor

The values in the market have changed. In the past they were mainly about competition and market dominance – very masculine values.

Today more feminine values of 'co-operation', 'co-llaboration', 'co-nnection' and 'co-mmunity' have replaced many of the old values.

Clients *want* to feel more engaged in the creation of their solutions, they *want* to be more a part of the process than ever before. They *want* more 'co-ownership' of their solutions.

They don't just want 'experts' telling them what they should do, - they want advisers who can engage, connect, advise and shape the very best of solutions for their needs.

Chapter 4: IQ v SQ

In the past business advisers and account managers often relied on their technical expertise, their IQ or 'intelligence quotient', to deliver a value to clients.

It was enough to be an expert or specialist, to come in and get the job done and then leave. Now, however, that is no longer enough.

Today clients expect that you are able to use your Social Intelligence (SQ or social quotient or intelligence) to create compelling and engaged relationships and demonstrate a real understanding of their concerns and fears - before they allow you to deploy your IQ or technical knowledge.

Our ability to deploy our SQ effectively ensures that we get the chance to deploy our IQ.

Often when I mention this in my coaching and seminar programmes delegates often reply that this doesn't matter when you are simply tendering for business, because it's just a process. However I reply that SQ, your ability to create and sustain a compelling engagement with the client, can be the difference that gets us the chance to tender in the first place, and may be the defining element when it comes to choosing between two similar tenders with two similar price points.

Today's relationship managers and business advisers are therefore required to have a significantly greater degree of understanding of the emotional dynamics that impact on relationships...and the most important of these - is trust.

Trust is a powerful thing, nothing moves and no-one acts without first having achieved some form of trust in a person or an undertaking. No directions are followed and no orders are placed without trust.

Trust is essential in business and what happens when trust is lost is that things spiral down to a stop and we face recession. Banks don't lend, businesses don't invest, jobs become insecure and consumers don't spend. In fact you could say that nothing moves without trust.

Trust is a function of rapport, and 'high trust' is a function of deep rapport.

Trust comes where there is first acceptance and where we have moved a business relationship, be it with a client or a key stakeholder within our own business, way beyond simply communicating with a person to where we connect, involve and engage with them on a personal and compelling level.

Where there is trust there is acceptance and where there is acceptance there is influence, then change can happen and decisions can be made.

The High Trust Adviser by Seán Weafer

Real trust in business is not from corporate communications or ad campaigns but from the work of the individual adviser, consultant, key account manager or sales professional, who builds it, one person at a time, colleague by colleague, client by client.

Business needs to return to being *transformational*, focused on people. Where engaging with the client becomes what it should be, not about the product or the service, but about the *experience* that the client gets from having engaged with us.

Growing our business depends on the quality of our relationships and this is an emotional art. Knowing how to manage a client's *emotional* responses is the key to managing their ultimate buying or business decisions.

Professional business development and account management is about the psychological and emotional dynamics of business, how well we can apply SI or 'social intelligence' or SQ 'social quotient' to business.

The basis of all business is in learning how to create compelling and collaborative client and staff relationships by creating and nurturing trust between us and the client and our staff.

After the market upheavals of the first decade of the century the need to continue to re-build trust in business, even today, means that we have to re-define our views and even our language about clients.

We have to start walking in the clients shoes, really start seeing things from their perspective and seeking to understand the values that drive the client's decisions.

Another element that is fundamental to the idea of 'high trust' business and which heightens the prospects experience is how we align the values of what we offer to the values of the client or prospect.

Values are global and abstract things - security, power, money, control, time and even harmony can all be defined as values. They can't really be explained or broken down any further, they are what they are and they each have a unique prioritisation and resonance with each customer.

However people do not share their values easily and sometimes aren't even sure what those values are. However by creating powerful rapport and trust with the prospect, by having them willingly accept us and our connection with them and then guiding them through a series of questions, we can rapidly identify and prioritise their key buying values.

By aligning a future client's unique values with the values of the service or the product that we are offering, we create a high trust, compelling business environment, we truly become high

The High Trust Adviser by Seán Weafer

trust advisers and executives and close more business with satisfied and life-long customers.

What I have termed 'High Trust Advisers' are the most in-demand professionals in today's competitive market.

After the radical damage to business relationships and the distrust inflicted by the collapse in the financial industry in the first decade of the new century, modern professionals must reach an even closer relationship with the client in order to build markets.

This requires a continuous review of our perspectives around business, our focus, our training and even our terminology, to allow us to build markets and trust in global business today, one person at a time.

The future of business is in the hands of well-trained High Trust Advisers.

There has been a radical change in business development in the first part of the century.

Now our prospects and client's do not need just information providers or 'brochure carriers' because today, they've got a much faster, portable and responsive Internet than ever.

Now they want us *to interpret* the information for them, to *advise* them on making the very best decisions for their business. They want us to understand where they are, to lead them forward and to walk the journey with them.

Unlike in traditional times today the buying cycle begins many steps ahead of the selling cycle.

The prospective client, by virtue of being able to access people's opinions through social media sites and peer-to-peer sites, often already has a good sense of what they are looking to buy long before they engage with a professional adviser or sales professional.

This means that they are better informed.

Therefore what they need now is someone who can *interpret the information* in a way that is meaningful and of value to them. They require not just a product or service anymore but *an experience* and we must create that experience from the moment that we meet with them.

In fact it begins even before we meet with them as we find a way to engage with them during their buying cycle, ensuring that we have a strong enough on-line presence to guarantee that we are the people they call when it comes to getting face to face with a supplier to discuss their needs.

Now is the time of the High Trust Adviser (HTA), old fashioned methods of just box ticking or process selling or bringing the brochures, just as old-fashioned and 'traditional sales training'

The High Trust Adviser by Seán Weafer

methods are over replaced by online learning and group coaching and mentoring.

High Trust Advisers understand the power of people over process...of SQ over IQ.

They are well versed in the relationship arts of influence, persuasion and psychology, and actively use technology to leverage their brand and their engagement in support of their clients.

They understand the power of networks and how to use networking opportunities so that they never have to 'cold call' a prospect but are welcomed into their offices and places of business.

They are re-defining the traditional global negative stereotype of traditional sales people as aggressive, pushy, self-interested and unprofessional, replacing it with one of professionalism, ethics, integrity and service to clients.

High Trust Advisers understand that business development and ethical selling is what creates and shares the wealth of nations and people and that commerce is what brings us together.

They understand that it is their work, the work of carrying the message to the world, that allows for the great inventions and advancements of science and business to be brought to the market and have a commercial life.

High Trust Advisers know that business development is a noble profession, that at its root are the principles of *service to others* and trust, and they are justifiably proud of what they do and how they serve their clients.

They also understand that knowing how to apply the dynamics of emotional intelligence in being of 'life time' service to their clients can help them get access to and the attention of key client decision makers so that they can create life-long and sustainable revenues.

In the next chapter we explore how our business messages have to be structured so that we become memorable in the mind of the client.

Chapter 5: The Million Dollar Message

If there is to be trust in business again it is the professional advisers and consultants, sales people, account managers, entrepreneurs - in fact anyone who has a revenue responsibility by getting face to face with prospects and clients - to re-build it one person at a time.

However there is a problem in client relationships today. They have become *transactional*, that is, process focused.

During the good years people and businesses spend, they come looking for us to give us their cash. Budgets are not a problem, only the spending of them.

Accountability is not as big an issue as it is when times are tougher.

Then client relationships became simply a matter of taking orders and we find ourselves with businesses where clients are managed by spreadsheet and not through real connection or engagement.

Client management needs to return to being *transformational* – focused on people. Where new sales and existing client relationships become what they should be - not about the product or the service - but about the *experience* that the client gets through having that product or service and that experience starts with 'first contact'.

'First contact' is the moment that we get in front of a prospect (and even long before that, in the form of our literature, our web presence and our reception staff), when their buying decisions are first beginning to form.

For me – 'first contact' is more powerful when it is face to face rather than over the phone.

A contact made when one has networked to meet them as opposed to 'cold calling' them is significantly more user friendly and open to engagement.

It's not that I am completely against cold calling or telemarketing but such traditional approaches to the market are proving less and less effective.

A High Trust Adviser on the other hand understands that all barriers that come between us and the prospect must be minimised. In addition he or she understands the dollar/pound/euro value of an hour spent wasted on the phone.

Here's a question – how many businesses have absolute faith in the quality of that 'first contact' with prospects? How many relationship directors or account directors or practice partners can, hand on heart, say that their people are consistently the best at creating compelling engagement with our prospects and our clients?

I'd say the honest answer is that we are back to 'the vital few' - Pareto's People - where 20% are doing 80% of the business.

Business development and especially 'selling' has for decades lived with being the poor step-daughter of business. It is an 'accidental' profession, people fall into it, nobody, when they are seven years old, chooses to grow up to be a sales person.

If we are a professional business adviser it has probably never been a required competency and our first experience of it was when we joined a practice or business. Yet today, *everybody must sell.*

However we do need to remind ourselves of the origin of selling.

It is said that selling evolved from the root word *'Selje'* meaning *'to be of service'*. So how many of us understand that we are in the business of being of service to our clients or customers?

The key to success and often the most difficult part of selling is getting the initial attention of prospective clients.

We do this by learning to forge what I term 'The Million Dollar Message'.

The High Trust Adviser by Seán Weafer

Re-building trust in business today may mean that we have to re-define our views and even our language about selling. More than ever we have to start seeing our services from the client's perspective and seek to understand the values that drive the client's decisions.

An example of this is our dependence on old terminology.

Everybody is familiar with the terminology USPs' – *Unique Selling Points*. In fact, everybody uses USP's. So many people use them in the same industries that they are no longer *Unique* Selling Points, they are *Generic* Selling Points.

It's because of this that I also believe that the idea of USPs (unique selling points) is terminology still used by 'traditional sales' professionals. High Trust Advisers use 'The Million Dollar Message'.

This is a message that is so compelling and so attention-grabbing that it sets us apart from everyone else chasing business with that client. It gets us noticed in the crowd, makes us memorable to the client, and opens the client to spending their budgets with us.

For years we've talked about USPs or Unique Selling Points by which we could differentiate our offerings and make ourselves stand out to prospective customers from the 'white noise' of competition.

The High Trust Adviser by Seán Weafer

The fact is that USPs *do not* make us stand out from the competition, in fact they only help to blend us in even further.

If we think about the USPs in any profession or industry can we really say that they are any different from what our competitors are also saying to the same prospects?

Do we sound exactly like our competition?

We provide 'solutions' or our 'experience' is second to none, we have 'one-stop-shops' or all the other *redundant terminology* that on any given day a prospect hears several times from different sales people.

A High Trust Adviser works on being memorable to the prospect. They sell to the prospects 'heart' and not to their 'head'.

They use what I call: **PCRs** and by that I mean '**Points of Compelling Relevance**'.

A **Point of Compelling Relevance** makes up the 'Million Dollar Message' – it makes the prospect want to act immediately on whatever it is that we are offering them. It makes them want to sign up NOW and commit *whatever* they have for whatever it is that we are offering.

USPs tend to appeal to the intellect or the reasoning ability of a prospect - it speaks to the surface of the sale - the *logical* benefits available by considering the offering. Prospects often have to work out the value for themselves.

However a PCR speaks directly **to the emotions or the feelings of the client where the benefit of the message is so relevant, so emotionally compelling** - that they buy now - the rationale is over-ridden in place of the emotion.

That emotion can be trust, power, money, time, profit, ambition, status, recognition but it is a *compelling* emotional trigger.

This is now where we can redefine 'selling' as:

'The ability to influence or heighten the emotional state of the client, so that we can influence their logical decisions for the transfer of goods, services or money for the mutual benefit of both parties'.

Of course, to create Points of Compelling Relevance requires more thought and testing than simple USPs and they tend to be unique to a particular prospect or prospect group, but the effect is immediate and unconditional. They buy...now.

A case in point was when I \worked with a bank's retail technology section, they had been asked prior to the workshop to bring their USP's to the table. Their big USP was that their 'credit card swiped twice as fast as any competitor'.

Amazing, there really was only one question one could ask about that - **'So what? What does that do for me - the client?'**

By working it through, and given that their key accounts were major retailers, we identified that the PCR was that *they could reduce queuing time for shop customers by 50% - thereby improving the customer experience of the store and aiding customer retention.* (They could also secure the transaction more quickly).

Do you think that *resonated* with their retail client? This became The Million Dollar Message that got them the access to, and the attention of, the client.

Taking the time to work through the real 'value to the client' that is buried deep within our industry or professional USPs allows us to uncover the language that most appeals to the emotional state of the client.

Once we discover the language that appeals to the prospects 'heart' (in actuality the unconscious, which is the seat of their emotions), rather than their 'head' (or the conscious part of the brain, which is the seat of their logic and analysis) we then shape it into powerful suggestions that make us memorable in the heart and mind of the prospect.

We create our unique Million Dollar Message.

For greatest effect the PCR language should be:

Concise - kept short and to the point rather than a rambling statement

Meaningful - relate to the powerful and personal benefit that the prospect can gain from our offer

Present Tense - the unconscious part of our brain responds best to instructions and suggestions made in the present-tense language rather than future-tense such as 'you will'. This is often why many personal goals fail as people frame them using the words 'I will' instead of 'I am' or I want to'

Simple - keep it simple, the unconscious, and hence our emotional response, is faster to respond when we keep the language simple

The result is a more engaged and informed prospect, one who is both powerfully and emotionally engaged in the pitch right from the start.

This is what creates the 'Million Dollar Message' in the mind of the prospect and our clients.

It helps us to stand out from the crowd of others chasing the market, get access to, and the attention of, the client, and unlock those Dollars, Pounds and Euros of life time revenue.

The High Trust Adviser by Seán Weafer

Now that we have our 'Million Dollar Message' our next chapter deals with how we take it to the market place in a way that gets us an 'invitation to sell'.

Chapter 6: How to Get 'Invited to Sell'

Being perceived as wanting to 'sell something' often creates a 'perceived threat' in the mind of prospects.

It is therefore important that we create a very favourable first impression and thus reduce the degree of resistance that we may have from prospective clients.

We want to make sure that we create a safe and non-threatening impression right from the very start of a relationship – when we first decide who we wish to connect with to create a business relationship.

By far the most effective way, in my experience, in creating valuable and qualified business prospects from a first contact is personal contact networking.

Therefore, today networking is not just an option, it is a professional requirement.

Why? Because in a world that is moving from old style command and control models of business to ones where *collaboration* is the key to success – one's network of contacts is a valuable asset.

It is increasingly recognised that the people who can leverage relationships are the ones who wield greater power in a world where information and access is critical.

The High Trust Adviser by Seán Weafer

Proactive networking can provide us with profile, position, credibility, market knowledge and the many other benefits of being able to work comfortably and consciously within a room full of other professionals and clients.

However having to "work the room" can be an uncomfortable, fearful and even resentful feeling for many of us.

Like the negative stereotypical image of 'the sales person' we often associate 'good networkers' with brash, self-confident people, who can handle any rejection, muscle themselves in anywhere and take over a conversation to suit their own ends - people that are not nice to be around.

We would rather hug the wall, cradling our coffees or drinks until we have waited the allotted time and can mercifully escape from this room of people who all seem to know each other.

However professional networking is about strategy, and fortunately, everyone can learn the strategy.

The first thing is to understand that networking is not about "selling ourselves" or pitching our company's offerings, and second is to understand that it's about *asking permission*.

Networking is not about us, it's always about the other person, a good networker will spend time asking questions and actively listening to what the other person has to say.

Not only that - but they will have reached this stage by having first gotten *the person's permission* to talk with them.

So what are the steps that get us speaking with not just anyone but the right person, the perfect prospect for my business?

1. Choose the Correct Event:
By this I mean select the event that is most appropriate to the profile of our ideal prospects.

Let me ask a question - where is the best place to meet professionals?

Answer…at their own events! With this basic understanding we can then start to choose the networking events we attend based on *profiling* or *niching* our clients.

By profiling our existing clients and dividing them into categories we can start to identify which client-types provide us with the most business.

Then it is a simple matter of identifying their professional associations, their suppliers associations, technical conferences – in fact anywhere they are likely to gather for reasons other than being 'sold to' by us.

For example, I was working with a well-known international accounting firm recently and one partner, using this profiling exercise, discovered *26 additional places* where her ideal prospect profiles met. That's 26 new opportunities where she and her team could access their prospects and renew existing client relationships.

However if we really want to excel at networking and establish as eclectic a network as possible my credo is simple **"wherever two or more are gathered together...there also shall I be"**.

Accept invitations to all events – plan them like a meeting and use them as tools to expand your contacts and influence.

Think about invitations as 'door openers' where someone else has done all the work to get us in the room with our exact type of client - to an event where everyone is a potential decision maker or referrer.

2. Target the People We Wish to See:
The more specific we are with networking the more successful we can be.

Plan out how many people we wish to meet (it's often best to go with a target of at least *three new contacts* per event). We can even plan to meet specific people who we know are at the event because of their value to us.

Ideally get the delegate list in advance from the event organiser - or get the attendee list when you get there.

With the delegate list secured before we attend the event we can now target specific prospects, and research them first on the Internet or on LinkedIn, which provides us with a photo and something of their background.

This can also help identify if we have any common connections or links who might provide an introduction.

…and it's not stalking …it's research!

3. Learn the Psychology of Networking

Conferences and seminars aren't just a morass of people. Next time we attend an event we should take time to study the room before we launch ourselves into the fray.

We'll then see that people arrange themselves in three distinct ways.

A. The Individual

B. The Open Group

C. The Closed Group.

A. **The Individual** will be just like us, on the edge looking for a way in.

They're wondering if they'll ever meet someone and how to go about it. These are a prime source of contacts and they really want to connect with someone. Anyone who says hello to these guys will be welcomed with open arms.

Remember that people come to networking events…to network!

To be accepted is the highest of human values. We are herd animals. So if we offer a chance to connect to the Individual then in most cases he or she is very likely to grasp it with open arms.

B. The Open Group is a collection of individuals – they don't really know each other so the group is arranged in such a way that there is always a space for another person to join at any time. This is our space; all we have to know is the secret of the introduction.

The best kind of Open Group to join is a mixed gender group – especially if we can make up the numbers. This is an opportunity to get many different contacts at one go.

C. Lastly the Closed Group. This group is best avoided because they know each other, they are in deep conversation and are not "open for business". They don't want anybody else joining.

Clever networkers also know that by joining an Open Group they can close the group to others until such time as they have "worked" the group and then they simply open the group again and disengage.

4. Making the Approach

So what is the magic formula that gets us 'invited in' to speak to all these people? Courtesy and permission.

On making the approach to an Individual or an Open Group, we first make eye contact and smile!

It's important to smile because a smile is a clear message to the other person's unconscious mind that we are harmless and therefore not a threat – as we humans cannot bite with our upper teeth alone, when the upper teeth are exposed we are communicating safety to the other person...

Then we ask ..."*Hi would you mind if I joined you?*" or '*May I join you?*'... we wait for the response (which will be positive), we then extend our hand to shake hands (another means by which humans install emotions) and join the person/group.

The key to engaging with anyone at an event is simply to request permission.

Ask – and you shall receive!

5. Ask Questions and Actively Listen

Most of us may have heard the phrase that in order to be interesting to people we must first be interested *in them*.

The High Trust Adviser by Seán Weafer

The very best way to keep people on side is to engage with neutral and open questions. These are questions which do not imply that a negative judgement will be made and are therefore seen as non-threatening.

A great way to start a conversation might be "What's your connection with the event" OR "How did you travel here?"

These neutral but universal questions engage a person in a non-threatening way allowing us to quickly establish rapport by relaxing that person in our company.

Key subjects to cover would be have they travelled far, how did they get here, how are they finding the event – then you can move to what's your connection with the event, then onto professional matters.

Keep the conversation focused on them.

Techniques such as the *Small Talk Stack* and others can help you learn to frame a conversation so that we are always on side with the person yet at the same time gathering vital information for future contact.

This starts with:

1. What's your connection with the event?

2. Where have you come from? Have you travelled far?

3. Pastimes or interests ('so what do you do when you're not networking?')
4. General topics such as current affairs or perhaps matter relating to the profession or the industry.

This kind of conversational structure ensures that:

1. We never run out of things to say and
2. The person we are speaking with feels both engaged and valued – which helps build rapport and trust.

When looking to spot business opportunities while networking questions such as:

1. Who makes the decision regarding our service or product within the firm?
2. Are they also at the event?
3. Would you be happy to connect me with them?
4. Who are they currently using?
5. How do they find them?
6. What are you most pleased with?
7. Where do you feel they could improve? (This highlights an opportunity for further work).

These questions will evolve naturally from when the other person quite naturally asks us 'what do *you* do?' – but remember that the question in the mind of the other person is really **'what can you do for me?'**

The High Trust Adviser by Seán Weafer

So our answer must always have relevance and value.

By the way please don't take this as an excuse to launch into a business presentation. This is the time for the elevator pitch – a short intro to what we do and how it could help them.

All of this is leading up to the point where business cards can be exchanged and permission (that word again) sought to make a contact call and 'arrange a coffee' - at a later date.

Such subsequent meetings then have the advantage of a "warm contact" made at the event followed by permission to call and so normally meet with a greater chance of accomplishing your objective from the contact.

When they give us their business card and we have agreed a time to call – always note the time and date of the call on the card. This provides a 'visual anchor' for the prospect indicating that we intend to call at the agreed time.

This then starts to create a 'double opt-in' with a prospect. The first opt-in is where they have given you permission to call them to invite them to coffee.

The second 'opt-in' is where – making absolutely sure that we call them on the day and the time we promised – they agree to have coffee and set a date and time to meet.

With the double 'opt-in' the prospect is now perfectly aware that they are going to have a business conversation about their issues. They have invited us to engage, identify their critical challenges and then suggest a viable solution.

This is low-pressure, high-permission networking.

There is also another simple but powerful strategy – which I call the **Advocate** strategy - for accessing more prospects using networking.

Many of us will have advocates – people who will happily speak on our behalf. People for whom our services or products have provided significant value and for whom we have delivered on one of the four key things that we sell:

1. We have saved them time.
2. We have saved them money
3. We have solved their problem
4. We have made them FEEL GOOD!

These advocates can serve as powerful sources of referrals for us provided we care for them.

I recommend that we list our advocates and create a strategy of advocate care – breakfast meetings, facilitating networking within the group, small gifts based on their interests and so forth.

The High Trust Adviser by Seán Weafer

Make sure that we connect with them on a business social networking site – LinkedIn tends to be the network of choice when it comes to business social networks.

By using this social media site we also get to see their second level of contacts, which are a rich source of potential referrals for us.

If our contacts are hiding them just politely enquire as to why – sometimes people aren't aware of the fact that they are hiding their contacts.

Personally, I have a policy of removing contacts from my LinkedIn contact list that deliberately do not allow me to see their contacts.

For me it is a policy that I've adopted that seems to get support.

LinkedIn is designed as a networking site and should be about people helping each other to reach out to each other's contacts - sharing and collaboration.

In a world where getting the attention and the time of prospects is getting harder LinkedIn can be a great tool for initial introductions.

However it can't work if people block or hide their connections from other people they are connected to. If you don't trust them to see your connections - why did you connect with them?

The High Trust Adviser by Seán Weafer

Access to your contacts allows me - through you and with your permission and support - to reach out to your contacts who I feel might benefit from my work.

If you have used me and value what I deliver then you should be happy to refer me (as someone that you know can do the job) to your own personal contacts and friends for their benefit.

To help with that introduction, I would typically send a short script that you could use and then you use the introduction facility on LinkedIn to put us in contact with each other.

I'm just looking for their permission to call them and get a meeting for coffee - once I'm there it allows me to research their needs and look at areas that I can bring value to them.

If I can't, I move on and thank them for their time (and buy the coffee!) and of course, I've asked permission to connect through LinkedIn if I haven't already.

If I'm referred to them through LinkedIn from a trusted contact of theirs - this gives me a visibility and trust factor right from the word go.

Just like being introduced to someone at a 'live' networking event - I get their attention and a higher chance of getting to meet them.

The High Trust Adviser by Seán Weafer

Networking is about trust and sharing and those that don't share don't get to play with me.

To be fair, and as I've already mentioned, people sometimes don't know that they have their settings set on LinkedIn to prevent their contacts being seen - and this is just a matter of ticking the box in the Settings section to make them visible.

But for those who deliberately keep their contacts private and aren't willing to share - it's like 'you show me yours but I won't show you mine' - sorry but I don't play that way. Transparency is king.

I have deliberately removed even good business acquaintances who are equally firm on their own policy of not allowing people to see their contacts. For me that just defeats the purpose of networking in the first place and serves no value to the wider community.

So as you grow your own networks do think about sharing and collaborating - it just makes for a bigger cake for us all.

But back to advocates - invite them to coffee or lunch – and while there ask them if they would be willing to introduce you to just three selected names that you have taken from their connections list.

Obviously the more advocates that we can create then the more personal referrals we get to have permission-based access to. 20 advocates could mean 60-120 new warm referrals in any given year.

No cold call, no push marketing- just an opportunity to create an 'invitation to sell'.

Now with the basics of networking behind us it's time to understand some of the etiquette or 'manners' associated with networking.

Chapter 7: Networking Etiquette

In the previous chapter, we covered a practical understanding of networking and its value to a professional adviser or key account manager in terms of creating the 'invitation to sell'.

We looked at the psychology of groups, of individuals, the approach and the kind of questions that we might use to open a conversation.

Here I'd like to cover the art of networking in a little more depth and explain how a simple conversation can be conducted to best effect....and how you can safely and ethically "park" someone when you have accomplished your objective.

When entering a networking arena, there are two things that one should keep in mind.

Firstly - everyone you meet is connected by at least six degrees of connection.

That is, that someone knows someone, who knows someone, who will eventually lead you to the person that you want to meet. So we should value all connections.

Everybody in that room should matter to us. Why? Because if we have done our research correctly and have entered the right room then everyone there is either a decision-maker or a potential referrer of business.

In networking – everybody matters.

Secondly, every single individual is there for the same reason as you, making connections that matter.

That means, that each person present is predisposed to meeting others and that each one of the people that we connect with are a link on a chain that can help us meet anyone else that we might wish to meet, provided that we follow the chain.

Let's deal with the second point, first.

Every single person there has two things in common with us, they have both travelled to be there and they have some connection with the event.

These are the two easiest things to talk about when we meet someone for the first time. When meeting someone and having made the approach and having once been accepted, we then have to ensure that we create rapport with that person.

Rapport is a sense of comfort and safety with others, our purpose therefore is to minimise any sense of threat that person may have about us, which is heightened by any sense of difference between us and them. Therefore we talk about neutral, open subjects.

The High Trust Adviser by Seán Weafer

By way of reminder from the last chapter, starting from the top, here are some sample questions to develop conversation with someone.

- What is their connection with the event?
- Where have they travelled from?
- How did they travel here?
- Where are they working?
- What do they do when they are not working (hobbies and interests) and finally
- Current, topical or professional affairs.

In between this of course, we need to find out about our own needs – like who are their current providers for your kind of service, what have they been most happy about with them (we always ask about the good stuff first so that we can assess their feelings about their existing providers).

Then ask if there are any areas in which they may be unhappy about the level of service.

Once we get a response, file it away and then return to the neutral questions.

Once we have carried on the conversation, we request their business card (if we haven't secured it already), ask them would they like to meet to discuss any area that we have identified in which we could be of service to them, over a coffee or lunch perhaps? (We are not selling here, *only getting permission* for a meeting).

As mentioned in the previous chapter we ask them when would be best to call and then note these details on their card, plus where and when we met them.

Now we have permission for a meeting and a warm contact with whom we have made a positive impression on, who is happy to engage with us at a future time. This is the best kind of contact. Remember it is also *essential* to call when you say you will! Your professional brand depends on it.

Once we have accomplished this one contact we then need to move on. Our objective at a networking event is to meet and get agreement from *at least three* people to meet after the event is over. So we need to know how to move on from them to our next contact.

Moving on professionally requires attention too. It is essential that we treat everybody we meet with respect.

Because we are all connected, we do not know who the person we are speaking with is connected to. How we treat them will determine how we are treated in the future by a possible excellent business contact. So, we NEVER dump – we 'park'.

We should never leave someone on their own when we move on but rather we should ensure that we have connected them with someone else. When someone feels that they have been abandoned by us they project that feeling onto us and are therefore not inclined to meet with us again.

Sometimes a contact is determined to "hang onto" us - perhaps fearful that they will meet no-one else if they let us go.

In either case we can disengage from a networking contact with the following method.

Just say *'I am going for a coffee...would you like to join me?'*

This might seem counter-productive but it is very important that we offer an 'out' to the other person. After all, they may have been trying to get away from us!

There will be one of two responses to our question:

1. They may say "No" – as they themselves are happy to move on at that point to meet someone else.
2. They may say "Yes" in which case, we would then *both* move to get a coffee.

Along the way, we scan the room for an Open group. Once located, we steer toward the group; introducing both ourselves and our new friend with the group – making the introductions where appropriate.

The High Trust Adviser by Seán Weafer

We have now introduced our original contact to new people, people they may never have met without our help.

We have helped them further their connections within an event that, up to our helpful intervention, might have been a complete waste of time for them.

The Law of Reciprocity ensures that they may therefore work harder at a later date to help us (Law of Reciprocity – you do something for me and I feel obliged to return the favour only to a greater degree).

After we have identified and engaged our preferred contacts from this new group and once we have determined the most suitable, we can then make our excuses and leave our original contact happily connecting with their new group of contacts.

It is simple, ethical and effective.

Networking is a requirement for all 21st business professionals, owners and relationship professionals. It is the means by which we build our networks of influence and promotion both within and without our organisations - and anyone can learn the strategies.

Next – how we make a powerful first impression at the time of 'First Contact'.

Chapter 8: First Contact

Creating Powerful Client Trust and Rapport

Rapport is *the* key to successful business relationships. Strong rapport means effective communication and a prospect open and willing to engage in taking the steps that effect lasting change in performance and development.

Exactly what rapport is has always been somewhat vague, many authors and trainers tend to gloss over it, somehow assuming that we should know instinctively how to create it.

That may seem to be a reasonable assumption. After all it *is* something we do quite naturally. But in just assuming that we instinctively know *how* to create rapport, we miss an opportunity to understand *what* it is that creates an influential relationship.

The starting point in understanding rapport is to have a definition to work from. So I've outlined below a possible definition with which we can work:

Rapport is that *state* in human relations where there is an agreed, sometimes silent, *recognition and acceptance* of common issues.

One of the key words in that description is the word 'state' – which can be defined as the emotional 'state' or 'feeling'.

Rapport *must* be present for there to be a high trust relationship in the first place.

We cannot expect to create a compelling relationship in which we have a strong degree of positive influence unless we are first masters of building deep rapport with a prospect or client.

Imagine a situation where we meet someone for the first time. What are our first feelings, are we immediately comfortable with them or are we unsure at first, cautious and perhaps a little suspicious?

Most likely the latter and this is perfectly natural. We seldom share our deepest secrets on first meeting someone. There is a process, mostly unconscious, which occurs within relationships as they develop.

However it's also true that we "click" with some people, while with others we take and maintain an immediate dislike to them. This is because at an unconscious level (and later at a conscious level) we have either positively or negatively been influenced by their appearance, language, voice, or behaviour and have sensed to a greater or lesser degree our shared or common issues.

In short, we have decided what level of threat to us this person represents by virtue of how different or how similar they are to us.

The High Trust Adviser by Seán Weafer

However, there are specific things which we can consciously use to ensure that we create the strongest rapport possible with people and so establish high levels of trust, respect and influential communication with them.

These are summarised in what I call the "*7-Step Rapport Process*". By using the elements of this we can quickly learn to create deep rapport with our prospects and clients.

These are all things that we mainly do unconsciously but by *consciously* understanding *what* we do *when* we do them, we can *"choose"* to use them in situations where we have to think about affecting a professional relationship.

It's also important to note that while this is broken down into a series of steps, they are all occurring in the first few minutes of meeting someone for the first time.

Step 1: Discounting

Within seconds of meeting someone we begin the process known as 'discounting'.

This is where we start to "mark people down" depending on their appearance, voice, body language etc. For each of us, we are the most 'perfect' person in our world, so we tend to compare everyone else *using ourselves* as the benchmark.

This process comes from our need to find out whether this person is a threat or a friend. This assessment is "hard-wired" into our brains from early in the development of mankind and is totally unconscious. It is only afterwards that we rationalise the decisions that we make.

This is how we begin to assess whether someone is similar to us and thus how open we feel that we can be with this person. This degree of openness has a direct effect on the level of rapport that we establish with someone else and ultimately the level of business that we eventually do with them.

This is why things like dress, appearance and body language have an important place in rapport as they are the initial points of reference that people use to ascertain their response to us.

The 'Secret of Rapport' is truly simple: *'People Like People - Who Are Like Them'*.

Therefore, the more like another person I can *appear* to be, the more likely they are to like me - and feel safe and comfortable in my presence.

As professional High Trust Advisers, we may have a need to adapt successfully to many different client styles.

By the time "Discounting" has been completed and the next stage begins we will have unconsciously critiqued the person we have just met and then moved to Step 2.

Step 2: *Judgement*

At this point we chose which "box" they go into. Humans need stereotypes to help them process the vast amount of information we receive whenever we meet someone for the first time.

We have 'mental templates' based on our past conditioning that other people are good or bad, attractive or not etc.

A great many of our relationships are based on this stereotyping or generalisation. It's one of the ways in which we process information and learn.

It's used extensively in film and TV as a means of being able to tell the story in a short time period. Can't we always tell the good guys from the bad guys in Westerns and soap operas – just by their dress or body language?

Now, the importance of understanding the power of rapport is this, while we are doing this to others, they are doing it to us.

It's useful to remember that judgement is a two-way process!

Therefore it is essential that our rapport-building skills are such that we are always assured of being marked in the upper percentile in other people's judgements.

Within two minutes or less of 'first contact' other people have decided whether we are a credible professional and so this is where we sow the seeds for a successful business intervention – or not.

Step 3: Eye-Contact
The 'eye's' have it.

Visually we immediately take in the appearance of the individual and we can often score major bonus points while communicating.

First, appearance is important. Suitable dress (appropriate to the circumstance), general hygiene, style of hair etc. will all help with the initial impact we make.

While we cannot always expect to be perfectly turned out on all occasions, remember that our clothes and general appearance reflects our professional or even social status and credibility.

More subtly, eye-contact or lack of it is also considered during the discounting process.

Poor eye-contact turns people off. It communicates poor (or lack of) interest in the other person.

No-one likes to be "overlooked" so they in turn reflect that back to us and exhibit a similar low level of interest in us, hardly the best way to start a High Trust relationship.

The High Trust Adviser by Seán Weafer

Generally, we should always maintain good eye-contact when we meet someone new. There is much to be said for having a good, open and honest gaze. The eyes are the windows of the soul and we can communicate very powerfully with just our eyes - when we flirt with someone for example or look skywards to portray exasperation.

However for some of us it can be difficult to maintain eye-contact without staring. This can be awkward as staring can often portray aggression or potential confrontation and most definitely will not assist us with developing good rapport!

In general, we create safe, neutral and yet effective eye-contact when we keep our gaze anywhere within an inverted triangle, with the apex ending at the point of the chin and the base of the triangle between the person's eyes.

Keeping our gaze anywhere within this imaginary triangle will help us maintain good, neutral but engaged eye contact of a non-confrontational nature while keeping the client's interest and attention on us.

Step 4: The Handshake
We can tell a lot about a person from a handshake, or at the very least we make assumptions about them, part of our discounting and judgement process which colours our dealings with them from that point on and hence our level of rapport.

A handshake can instil feelings in someone about us as soon as 'first contact' is made. As most client decisions are emotionally-based, we need to ensure that first feelings are good feelings.

For example, how do we feel when we get that loose, limp, "wet fish", disinterested handshake which hardly passes as a handshake at all? Or what about the "earthquake" where the hand is seized and squeezed in a vice-like grip?

Sometimes clients may attempt to dominate the handshake (and hence the relationship) and their hand will be very prominently placed, palm downwards, on top of ours, deliberately (although probably unconsciously) placing us in a submissive position. They may even extend their hand with theirs pointing downwards, forcing us to place our hand underneath theirs.

To counteract this, all we have to do is cover the top of their hand by grasping it briefly with our other hand, so that we end up enclosing their original handshake in our two hands.

Now who's in charge.....and we have given a clear sign that we intend to conduct our business and relationship as equals.

However, we can also use this in our favour.

By being the first to engage someone by extending *our* hand *palm upwards* in the "submissive" position – we immediately place our client in a "dominant" (and therefore more secure and 'in control') position.

Their immediate feelings are therefore of being in control, safe and as a result their initial anxiety or initial sense of threat is lessened - as is their potential resistance to us.

Step 5: The Power of Your Smile
Smiling is critical when meeting someone for the first time. It conveys an attitude of openness and acceptance to the person, helping them to relax and to be open to us in turn.

Think of the last time you met someone....where they smiling or not?

How did it make you feel the last time you met someone who smiled as if delighted to meet you? Now think of how that makes others feel when *you* meet them.

For ourselves, it helps us to relax and places us in a positive state, which makes it easier for us to manage the communication. The better and more relaxed we feel the easier the conversation will be.

In addition, our expectations of the success of the conversation will be high. Such expectations cause a reciprocal effect from the other person and hence the process tends to be successful.

The single greatest human need is that of *acceptance*, and it is conveyed easily and effortlessly with the power of our smile. Smiles are infectious too, they just seem to spread good cheer and warmth into a relationship.

Smiling comes from the fact that by exposing our upper teeth we are indicating that we cannot attack, primarily because (as humans) we cannot grasp with our upper teeth alone.

However if we stick out our chin and expose our lower teeth, we are indicating hostile intention. Ever notice someone getting aggressively hostile? They immediately stick out their chin don't they? They unconsciously intend to "take a bite" out of us.

Smile.

It's great for our health and gives us the upper hand in communicating with others, and smile with your whole face, not just your teeth. There's nothing worse than an insincere smile. It's an effort to create and does not help the relationship in anyway. People know whether we are being sincere or not.

From a more technical point of view a genuine smile can be distinguished from a forced one because the muscle that raises the cheeks causing those "crow's feet" or "smiling eyes" only contracts when people are expressing the true emotion of happiness.

The High Trust Adviser by Seán Weafer

Smiling can save us great points on the discounting scale and it's fun to do.

Step 6: Intelligent Questions

As a skilled professional adviser, consultant or key account manager it's important for us to remember that *the person who controls the questions is the person who controls the conversation.*

It's also important to remember that, in general, people love to talk about themselves. *They* are *their* favourite subject. So *let* them.

It's not often that we get an attentive audience and we tend to love the opportunity to talk about ourselves. We also tend to think very favourably about the people who listen attentively to *our* stories.

So, ask them questions. It's a powerful rapport-building tool. It enhances the client's feeling of safety with you, as the person they are hearing the most is themselves – and who do they feel the safest and most comfortable with? Themselves.

Questions maintain attention, allowing us to identify the triggers by which clients make their decisions, the values that they consider important; they allow us to install ideas, explore, change perception. They are the ultimate influencing and 'High Trust Adviser' tools.

We'll cover this further in the chapter on Advanced Questioning Skills.

Step 7: Body Language

Body language lends a great deal to the *congruence* (or the "rightness") of our message.

People will always look at the body language before they listen to the spoken word and will act on this first, when it comes to making decisions about the validity of your message.

If, for example, we are stretching and yawning while at the same time telling people how wonderful it is to be here with them, and how exciting we find their company - they're not likely to be convinced of the sincerity of our message, are they?

So a great deal of the sincerity of the message will be tied up in how our body is reacting (or not) to the people with whom we are communicating. Body language is too great a subject to explore here - but here are some simple tips:

1. Be aware of your distance from your prospect or client – breaching a client's privacy barrier will cost you points on the rapport scale. Too close and they may feel intimidated.

2. However, some people have a need for a great deal of space between themselves and others – noting how far or

how close they come when shaking hands with you can give an indication of what's safe and not.

3. Touching a client can sometimes help anchor encouragement or praise.

   However the body has "neutral" and "hot" areas that we must be aware of. For example, the arm from elbow to shoulder is "neutral" or acceptable to touch – the arm from elbow to hand is not as it may be considered intimate and inappropriate.

4. Mannerisms: Mannerisms are those unconscious habits which we all have to some extent.

   They are not just physical but can also be verbal - for example the person who continually ends each sentence with the words "eh?" or "you understand" or "actually" or "you know" or some form of words of which they are totally unaware but which the listener is getting increasingly tired of hearing.

5. Mannerisms can also be physical - the constant tapping of a foot or finger for example. In each case they should be identified and removed from our physical behaviour.

   But how do we remove something that is unconscious? Pluck up the courage to ask our partner or spouse the things they notice about us – I could guarantee that the things they notice and are willing to comment on, are the same things strangers and work colleagues notice, but say nothing about and simply file away in the compartment of their views about you.

6. Posture: Posture, or the way our bodies stand or sit or lie, often reflects our inner state or how we are feeling at any time.

   For example, travelling to work on a Monday morning, do we notice the posture of most people passing us by? Usually unhappy about returning to a job they no longer enjoy or find interest in, they tend to have a "hang-dog" look about them. Their heads are down, their bodies slumped.

   But notice these same people on a Friday afternoon. Work is over for the week. They're laughing, heads high and looking forward to time for themselves. Their bodies are reflecting the up-beat mood that they are experiencing internally.

Sports people often use "physical determination techniques" – going through a series of exercises prior to a game to get both their minds and bodies ready for the athletic challenge ahead.

The High Trust Adviser by Seán Weafer

So in the process of communication with prospects and clients, what state should we ideally be in - upbeat or depressed? Can't we often tell how someone feels just by the way they appear?

We need to be more conscious about our own body language and the message it's giving to the people with whom we wish to communicate successfully.

Let's face it – few people want to socialise with manic depressives, they want to socialise with people who generate a sense of confidence in and comfort with themselves. So by being conscious of our body language we can send a powerful and unconscious message to those around us.

Body language too plays a part in the processes of matching and mirroring.

Matching and mirroring are the means by which we reflect back to people their own postures and actions. The purpose behind this is to indicate that we are like them.

Remember the 'Secret of Rapport': People like People Who Are Like Them? So, the more we can match the physical behaviour of others that we want to influence, the more like them we appear to be, the more likeable we can appear to them.

Matching is the process by which we copy the actions of the people with whom we are communicating.

As a very simple example, if we are facing someone and they raise their left hand, then we raise our left hand. If they cross their legs, then we cross our legs. It's very similar to the game children play which drives adults nuts when they do it to us.

Mirroring is similar to matching in that we wish to convey like behaviour – but the difference is that instead of moving exactly like the other person, we now move in the reverse.

If they move their left hand we move our right, if they move their right leg, we move our left.

The purpose behind this is that we now appear to the other person as if we were appearing as their reflection in a mirror to them and therefore appear to be doing exactly what they do. This can create very deep rapport indeed, even to the extent that the person may believe that the words that we use are their thoughts!

But a word of caution: the secret behind matching and mirroring is that they must be done out of the level of the other person's conscious awareness and out of synch with their movements…never at the same time as the client.

The High Trust Adviser by Seán Weafer

Ever notice kids doing it to us and it drives us nuts, how would other adults feel if they notice us doing it to them? This is called 'mimicking' – not an appropriate use of body language!

There is sufficient knowledge in the public arena available to people to know why we might want to match and mirror them – and no-one likes to feel they are being manipulated. So if it's obvious that we are doing it, what are the consequences?

Timing and subtlety are therefore crucial in applying matching and mirroring techniques.

So here are some useful guidelines:

Match and Mirror the Parts of the Body that You and the Other Person See.
There's no benefit in matching/mirroring if the other person cannot see the actions, if it does not register, it's wasted.

Actions Should Be Offset by Timing
If someone is using their hands when speaking to us, stay still. When they stop speaking and we start to speak then we can match that action. Likewise if they lean forward, take your time, then say something and lean forward to match the posture of the other person.

They are both focused on and distracted by what we are saying and generally will not consciously notice that we are using (or "feeding back") their gestures to them.

Pace, Pace, Lead, Lead
This is how we can identify if we are generating rapport with someone.

Pacing is when we are following the actions of the other person. We would continue to do this until such time as we get a sense or a feeling that we are in rapport.

To test this, we would then change the pattern of pacing by moving or making a gesture of our own. If the other person then follows us, we are in rapport and we can then lead that person through our own gestures and movements.

As long as the other person then continues to follow our lead, they will be open to the suggestions or ideas that we wish to present to them.

Rapport with Two or More People
When generating rapport with more than one person, it is sometimes necessary to focus on one while matching or mirroring the other(s). The person that you want to match or mirror should be the dominant one within the group.

You can match/mirror the dominant person's actions while paying specific attention to the other people in the group. By doing this, we are generating rapport in two ways.

Firstly we are creating "first level" rapport with the dominant member of the group through posture. This should bring them closer to us and unconsciously into rapport and thus agreement with what we are saying.

This person is unaware of our actions because we are not directly facing them or perhaps only occasionally addressing them, while we are in fact appearing to concentrate our attention on the other people in the group.

By doing so we are then taking on some of their authority within the group – by appearing like them.

This then lends authority to our communication with the other members because we are now communicating with the "likeness" of the dominant group member or through "second level" rapport.

Positioning

Another important aspect is the way we position ourselves when we seek to match/mirror people. Where possible, we should try to avoid sitting directly opposite someone. We need to try and offset our seating arrangement so that our chair is at a 45-degree angle to the person with whom we are seeking to create rapport.

This has two effects. One, it appears less confrontational and two, it limits their perception of the fact that we may be matching/mirroring their movements and actions.

Remember, we only get one chance to make a first impression.

Therefore, professional High Trust Advisers use all the tools at our disposal to ensure that our first impression is the very best possible.

'First Contact' with a prospect or client can make all the difference in creating a long-term, mutually profitable business relationship.

Once we have made 'first contact' the next stage is how to consciously deepen the level of rapport.

By learning how to work with the unique client personality types that we meet every day, and by being able to 'flex' our style to appear more like the client, we can learn to deepen trust and maximise influence.

It's time for 'Selling in Colour'.

Chapter 9: Selling 'In Colour'

Imagine a situation where, within a few minutes of meeting a prospect or client, we could read their personality preference *and* be able predict the way they were likely to respond to us, and *then* adapt our own responses to match theirs and thus create powerful and deep rapport and trust?

Think of the benefits.

One could choose *exactly* how to respond to them, *match* their communication style, know *how* to feed them information in the *exact way* in which they process information, know *exactly* how quickly they were likely to make decisions and what makes them *comfortable* when communicating.

As a High Trust Adviser we need to go beyond just communicating a message. We must have the ability to *connect* with, to *involve* and to *engage* others at a deeper level as this is what can determine the degree of our success or failure with any given prospect or client.

Understanding some of the psychology behind connecting with others gives us a powerful means of creating rapid rapport and deepening trust.

This chapter introduces a highly-effective (and fun) model for communications excellence based on the many 4-Quadrant behavioural systems that are available in the market as a training tool today.

For centuries, philosophers have identified four broad types of personality. Over 2,500 years ago the Greek philosopher and medical pioneer Hippocrates was the first to be credited with typing human behaviour and providing the first colour system which we still draw from today.

The eminent psychotherapist Dr. Carl Jung further developed this idea in the 20th century and added his own concepts on how we focus our energies, make decisions and whether we are big picture (global) thinkers or specific thinkers.

Jung suggested that we have the capacity for all kinds of personality traits or energies within us, but that we have a preference for exhibiting certain traits above others.

It is this balance of energies or personal traits (or 'functions' as he called them) that makes each of us unique, and while we may share some (or even many) traits with others, we are all unique creatures, with unique preferences.

The full range of psychological types can be depicted (as per Hippocrates) as a circle with four key colour quadrants – Red, Yellow, Green and Blue. I also refer to them as the Warrior, the Entertainer, the Healer and the Mystic.

The High Trust Adviser by Seán Weafer

All of us have one of these as a "dominant colour preference" which gives us a preferred style of thinking, working and interacting with others.

Each colour preference or personality type has its own unique strengths and weaknesses, depending on the situation and the perspective of others.

There is also sometimes a slightly less dominant (but still strong) colour preference, or secondary colour, which can also impact significantly on our behavioural style.

To make matters even more interesting, when mapped using a psychometric profile, we can see that most of us can have *two* distinct styles of personality.

We have an *'unconscious'* style or preference which is our natural self or *'who we are when we are not thinking about who we are'*, our 'unmasked selves' or what I sometimes call our 'default setting' self. This is often what family and close friends see.

Then we have our *'conscious'* self, which is the 'mask' or the communication preference style that *we choose to project to others when we go to work*.

These personality preferences come down to how the colours on the quadrant interact with each other – some being closely aligned and others being polar opposites.

However the real secret is in recognising that the traits are not opposite but complement each other and a successful High Trust Adviser can recognise this and use it to their advantage and that of the client by creating a close, compelling and open relationship.

Now let's look at the four key prominent colours or personality types and the traits that we can associate with them:

REDS (The Warrior) tend to be direct and up-front, quick to make decisions and very focused.

They come across as probably the most seemingly confident of the colours, having a high degree of 'inner certainty' which means that once they are happy with an idea they seldom look to others for affirmation that it's the right thing to do. They just do it.

They are very determined and love to face a challenge. Being action-oriented they tend to *'reflex rather than reflect'* – which works for them but can be quite a challenge for other colours.

They can be very articulate and tend to be 'big picture' thinkers – not great on the detail but very good at creating the vision or the mission.

For their opposite colour however – *Green (The Healer)* - they can often appear as aggressive or arrogant, not waiting for feedback and pushing others too hard.

The High Trust Adviser by Seán Weafer

They would be considered as a poor listener, confrontational and not waiting for feedback or valuing the contribution that others make.

Some Greens (Healers) might even consider a Red (Warrior) to be a 'bully'.

What lies behind this however has to do not just with the preferred values of the Red but also their *style of communication*.

Being 'Visual' communicators they 'see' things and, as a picture paints a thousand words, they feel that they have to describe in detail what they are seeing.

As they 'see' a new mental image every nanosecond this requires a lot of information that has to be transmitted, meaning they can overwhelm people who do not process in pictures but in some other form of modality (such as Greens or Healers who process information by *feeling or touch)*.

Reds (or Warriors) often benefit from learning *to ask more questions*, and *making more suggestions*, *slowing their speed* of communication and allowing others to have the chance to engage with them.

Equally when we are communicating with a Red (Warrior) we need to speed up our own pace of speech. Only then can the Reds (Warriors) receive the information at a speed that they can create the mental imagery necessary to make sense of things.

In fact it is by learning to be able to *flex our preferred communication style* that we connect successfully with the other colours.

This may seem uncomfortable and require some effort on our behalf, especially when dealing with an opposite colour, but it does help significantly to make the other colour more comfortable with us, bringing down barriers, lessening threat and increasing their capacity to engage.

The values, or buying motivators, of a Red tend to be power, status, ambition and control.

For Reds (Warriors) 'control' is an important value and they often need to see that we are 'in control' of things when we work with them as advisers.

If we fail to keep them 'in the communications loop' on things, if we fail to let them 'see' us regularly, even just popping in and updating them on things, they quickly move to micro-managing us, fearful that we are not 'in control'.

Some people fear challenging the opinions of Reds, believing this will lead to confrontation or aggression.

The High Trust Adviser by Seán Weafer

In fact most Reds (Warriors) positively welcome 'push back', especially if it adds to the information that allows them to get the task or the mission done. So stand your ground and be firm, just never challenge them for position or power.

Reds (Warriors) can make very good clients.

Usually they have the authority (as their ambition moves them up the ladder) and they make decisions quickly. Once the decision is made they tend to stick with it.

We just need to keep our presentation and meetings short, positive and focused on the subject. The most effective strategy for influencing them is simply to let them think it's their idea!

Recognising a Red (a Warrior) is done by knowing that they are:

1. Extroverted and tend to speak at a fast pace.
2. Task (not People) Focused, interested in logic, data, and accomplishing the mission.
3. Global or 'Big Picture' thinkers.

YELLOWS (Entertainers) are highly sociable and love the concept of fun, recognition and variety.

Fun and interacting with others are key parts of their personality, and they tend to be happy to spend lots of time with visitors. They can be demonstrative, enthusiastic and very expressive, often finding their way into creative and media industries.

Like Warriors they are extroverted and articulate but they are less well organised or focused.

In fact, meetings with Yellows (Entertainers) will tend to last longer than other colours as they love to chat about everything and anything, but often need to be gently brought back time and again to the point of the conversation!

Yellows (or Entertainers) process information through *sound* and as a result are not great readers. They prefer to communicate *through conversation rather than writing*.

They are quick to build relationships, can often be seen as 'chatty' and 'the life and soul of the party', in fact if they walk into a room and there is no-one there they are likely to end up talking to the wall, as they just can't prevent expressing themselves!

Rather than long written proposals Yellows would prefer to be *talked through* the proposal, their primary processing modality being auditory or sound.

They are highly adaptable and people-focused but tend not to be good at organisation, planning or detail.

The High Trust Adviser by Seán Weafer

Like the Reds they are Global thinkers, great with the origination of an idea, often highly creative but they tend not be very good completer/finishers of projects.

As a result, they may travel down many pathways with us but getting them to make a final decision to buy can be a challenge. Without arranging to walk them through a proposal, this same proposal may sit in an 'in' tray and never be looked at again!

They also tend to make decisions quickly and then either forget they made the decision or fail to follow-up.

Their buying values tend to focus on fun, recognition and variety.

For them their greatest challenge is in communicating with the highly reflective, detail-focused Blues.

Blues (Mystics) tend to see Yellows as excitable, frantic and even indiscreet (!) and can be challenged when dealing with their upbeat and outgoing natures. A Yellow (Entertainer) might find a Blue (Mystic) cold and reserved, unwilling to engage and become part of the group, preferring their own company.

Recognition can be a great driver for them and Yellow personality types can be most open to corporate entertainment, as they like 'to see and be seen'.

Recognising a Yellow is done by knowing that they are:

1. Extroverted, as they display strong extroverted behaviour and speak in a medium to fast pace.
2. People Focused (unlike the Reds who are Task focused), interested in how people feel and figure in the scheme of things.
3. Global or 'Big Picture' thinkers.

GREENS (the Healers) are tremendous listeners and highly supportive of others.

Being of service to others is important to them, and they can be patient, polite and pleasant to all that they meet.

They are caring and encouraging of others, somewhat reserved, patient and relaxed.

They process information through how they *'feel'* about things, and such a modality means that they can often *take longer to make decisions* as they need the time to reflect on their physical feeling about an idea or a proposal.

Greens (Healers) can be slower to respond to a question or a suggestion as they process the information *kinaesthetically* (through feeling), wanting to be *comfortable* with any response before they give it.

The High Trust Adviser by Seán Weafer

This can often frustrate a Red (a Warrior), or even a Yellow (an Entertainer), who are used to making quick decisions and want things to move along quickly to suit *their* preferred communication style.

However a Green might find the Red arrogant and aggressive, the Red Warrior's sense of inner certainty, confidence and task focus at odds with the Green Healer's more collaborative and team-based style.

The way a Green feels about things is very important indeed. The worst thing that one could do is force a Green into making a decision, without allowing them time to 'get a feel for it'.

Doing so can result in the Green (Healer) preference person being so uncomfortable that they could cancel an order or contract or even end the business relationship.

Usually I recommend to others that before a meeting with a Green Healer, where a decision might be required, that all relevant and written documentation be sent to them *ahead of any meeting* to allow them to review, get a feel for it, and prepare for the face-to-face meeting.

For Greens their key values, around which they would base their buying decisions, would be loyalty, trust, transparency, stability, security and comfort.

As we can see from some of these values they are not clients who are quick to change providers and would only do so if they feel very 'uncomfortable' or 'uncared for' with and by the existing provider.

For Healer's the quality of the relationship is critical. They are highly people focused and expect to be valued and listened to.

Recognising a Green Healer is done by knowing that they are:

1. Introverted, as they display relatively introverted behaviours. They tend to speak at a slower and reflective pace, seeming a little reserved towards others in early interactions.
2. People Focused, (unlike the Reds who are Task focused), interested in how people feel and figure in the scheme of things.
3. Specific thinkers, (focused on the small details and the specifics).

Finally our **BLUES** (or Mystics) are highly-analytical, reflective, thoughtful people who like to make effective decisions based on a sound understanding of the situation or data.

They are the kind of person who prefer to reflect and seek to understand even the smallest of details before committing to any decision.

The High Trust Adviser by Seán Weafer

This can often mean that not only are they slow to confirm or make a decision, but they can be seen as strong procrastinators, waiting too long to make decisions.

Of course once the decision is made they are absolutely committed to it and become very unlikely to change their mind in the near future, so they often make long-term clients.

They tend to process information through what we call an Auditory Digital process. In its simplest form this means that they like to have a conversation in their own minds about things before they talk to the person actually having the conversation with them!

This is why the Blue Mystics are sometimes called 'low reactors' in relationships, remaining silent and reflective and allowing the other person to do the talking. In fact they are having a conversation, but with themselves.

They love information in writing, preferring to analyse information, and one cannot provide them with enough data.

Their values are order, organisation, stability, systems and planning, and are very comfortable with numbers, often making excellent administrators, accountants, engineers, technical people, actuaries and so forth.

They will ask (a lot of) questions and as *credibility* is also a key value for them it is important that we are well versed in our subject matter, or bring someone with us to the meeting who is, as they will ask very technical and detailed questions. No point asking them to read the manual – they already have!

There is no way that we can expect to muddle our way through a meeting with them. If we don't have the information or can't answer the questions they will quickly switch off, seeing you as wasting their time.

Like the Green Healers, but even more so, it is a useful strategy to send a lot of information in advance of any meeting, and then email them to request a list of questions they would like us to address during the meeting itself.

This kind of pre-meeting preparation will ensure a much more favourable response from the Blue, and ensure that we get to a positive decision sooner.

Recognising a Blue Mystic is done by knowing that they are:

1. Introverted as they display relatively introverted behaviours. They tend to speak at a slower and reflective pace, seeming quite reserved towards others in early interactions – even more so than a Green Healer.
2. Task Focused (unlike the Yellows who are People-focused), interested in logic, data, rationale and the task or measureable objective.
3. Specific thinkers (very focused on the small details and the specifics).

The High Trust Adviser by Seán Weafer

When we can understand the principles of this colour model we move from a world of 'black and white' (I like you or I don't like you) to one of 'glowing rainbows of colour', quickly and elegantly able to recognise, adapt and build high levels of trust with our clients or key stakeholders.

Success in today's world is about a different set of values from than those that mattered in the past.

Now the values of business are collaboration, co-creation, connection and community, and all of this begins with our ability to act with greater awareness or consciousness when we meet others.

This is the mark of a High Trust Adviser.

In the next chapter I explain how we can actively influence clients now that we have learned how to build powerful and deep rapport and trust.

Chapter 10: Advanced Questioning & Influencing Skills

As children nothing came more naturally to us than the powerful "WHY?" question.

"Why is the sky blue Daddy?" – "Because the angels painted it that way love" – "Why is the grass green Daddy?" – "Because the angels painted it that way munchkin" – "Why did the angels paint it that way?" – "I don't know love - go ask your mother…!"

Questions are powerful tools for influential communication. They can serve to instil ideas in people's minds, change their perception of problems, and help us to gain compliance or agreement to our suggestions.

As skilled professionals, it's important for us to remember that *the person who controls the questions is the person who controls the conversation.*

It's also important to remember that, in general, people love to talk about themselves. They are *their* favourite topic. So let them.

So, ask prospects questions. It's a powerful rapport-building tool. Get the prospect involved, and more importantly get them involved in **co-designing** their own solutions.

The High Trust Adviser by Seán Weafer

The more a prospect is involved in solving their own problems, with our help, then the more ownership they take of the solution and the less likely they are to walk away from a proposal that we build together.

Another key reason for our using questions is that when a client or prospect are looking to answer our question, it is at that moment, more than any other moment in the conversation, that they are focusing their full attention, involvement and engagement on us, our proposal or our service.

They are just not thinking about *anything* else at that time.

The most common types of questions used within the selling or consulting process are the **Open** question and the **Closed** form of question.

The Open question is one that encourages a person to talk. It is designed to gather information, opinions, thoughts and ideas. The British writer Rudyard Kipling had a little verse that summed up the key forms of Open questions:

"I had six honest serving men and they served me true. Their names were How, What, Where, Why, When and Who"

By using these six questions we can gather enormous amounts of information from people during the course of a single conversation - whether of a business or personal nature.

Open questions however can be answered by unqualified or unspecified answers. For example 'how many people are coming to the meeting?' might be answered by 'a few' or 'about ten'.

However by using the word **'specifically'** in the question this ambiguity can be removed every time. 'How many people – *specifically* – are coming to the meeting?' would be answered by 'the CEO, CTO and CFO' or 'exactly 5 people'.

Closed questions on the other hand are designed to elicit either a Yes or No answer. They are not designed to encourage conversations. They are designed to get confirmation of information.

These questions are typically *Did, Is or Are?*

Having now looked at the basic open and closed questions, here are some examples of more sophisticated types of questions.

Tag Questions

Tag questions are questions that can be added to the end of a sentence, buried in the middle of a sentence or hidden at the start of a sentence, and they are used to elicit a positive response, or "yes" answers, from people.

I mean, if you were to ask your client to get a positive answer you would wouldn't you? Couldn't you? If you wanted to you,

The High Trust Adviser by Seán Weafer

don't you think you could just get a positive answer by asking a simple question? Of course you could, couldn't you?

Words like wouldn't, can't, don't, shouldn't, doesn't and so on are ideal tag questions and such questions are usually used *after a suggestion to take an action has been made using an Open question.*

First the suggestion...followed by a tag question...which receives the affirmative response and confirms the suggestion as agreeable to them.

'Perhaps we could now just *get the paperwork out of the way*? That would be worth considering *wouldn't it*?'

Preferential or 'Double-Bind' Questions

Preferential questions pre-suppose that the listener, once presented with the question, accepts the offer or the option inherent in the question. It's just a question of *which* option they are accepting.

For example, "would you like to go now or in 30 minutes?" pre-supposes that the individual *is* going, even though they may not have considered it *before* the question was asked. They just have a choice over *when* but not *if* – hence the 'double-bind'.

"Would you like me to call tomorrow or the next day" is a useful and common preferential question for setting up appointments.

Such questions involve an option, but one that works in our favour, regardless of which option the listener chooses. We control the options but they have a choice of which option to take.

This is important as offering too many buying options to a client can be confusing and lead to delay – offer them two no more than three options at the most at any time.

Exploratory Questions

Exploratory questions are a development of the open question type.

They are useful when we are seeking clarification or further information about the subject raised by another person, or in answer to a question from another person.

The question is asked as follows: **"How** Do You Mean?" which has a number of benefits for us.

The first is that we get clarification on the meaning of the communication (for example a statement or question) raised by the other person.

This happens because asking the question causes a person to "go inside" themselves and re-frame the question or statement so that it has a greater clarity for the listener (us).

They then will re-state the question to us in the new format, making it clearer for us to understand.

The other benefit is that, while they are re-considering their own question, we also have more time to consider *our* response.

It's worth noting that the question 'How Do You Mean?' is actually grammatically incorrect.

The more usual form of such a question is "**What** Do You Mean", which requests a much more specific answer. However if you ask someone '**what**' do they mean it is likely they will say exactly what they just said and not take the time to explain it or re-interpret what they originally said.

It is the asking of **"How"** that causes the other person to re-frame and re-consider their initial question or statement.

Answer-Assist Question

What happens when someone says 'I don't know' in answer to one of our questions?

Often it tends to end the conversation and we have to find another way to raise the subject.

Most people answer 'I don't know' for three different reason:

1. They have an answer but are concerned that they might be criticised on the response and so keep it to themselves.
2. They genuinely don't know the answer.
3. They don't wish to give an answer because they are trying to block further discussion on that subject.

Our response to an 'I don't know' answer would then be to say:

*"I completely understand how you might be unsure at the moment BUT **if you <u>were</u> to know or <u>suppose</u> you knew** what would you say or what would you do….?"*

The key here is "**if you were to know or suppose you knew**".

This takes the person out of their current limited perception of the problem and allows them to search their full internal resources to come up with a solution.

Most people have understanding and knowledge available to them far beyond what they may be consciously aware of, but most of this is stored at an unconscious level.

By asking the question "if you were to know" or "just suppose you knew" or if "you could imagine a solution, what might that be", we give them a key to access that unconscious information from where it is stored in the brain.

At this point a person who had some uncertainty about sharing a response will share it with us, as the question also removes any sense of negative judgement being made on their answer.

In the case of a person who has no response because they still genuinely don't know or continues to block us by again answering 'I don't know' then we continue to move the process forward by taking control and saying:

'In that case …may I make a suggestion…?'

The person who is genuinely stuck will gratefully accept the suggestion while the person who is attempting to block us must either also accept the suggestion or reveal their reasons why they are not willing to engage on the topic with us.

Internal Representation Question
An internal representation question allows you to influence the mood someone is in.

We know that people *literally* see the world differently when they are in different moods, so we want them in the most positive mood possible when dealing with us don't we?

For example, we want a customer to associate a positive feeling with our service or product so we might ask – *"Can you remember a time..* when you bought something you were really happy with, something that really pleased you, can you remember that item, a specific one?

This causes the client to associate back to that experience, re-establishing that good feeling in the client and as we see them begin to smile and their physiology or body language shift (as it will) we then ask and "wouldn't it be great to feel that way again and this could just do that for you couldn't it." (Note the tag question?).

Don't you think we just might have their attention? It's just possible that we have that positive, receptive, feeling that all professionals know is the right mood for making a decision?

Equally we could also use it in a situation where we wanted to create a positive response from people to us personally.

Can you remember a time when you felt absolutely relaxed and confident with someone? A time when you knew you were learning from a professional and you could see all the benefits that would come from the learning, can you remember a specific time – now? And wouldn't it be nice to feel that way again.

A High Trust Adviser understands the power of being able to influence the emotional state of the client and the impact they can create by heightening their emotional responses and thus influence their conscious decisions.

Listening Skills

Another key element in influencing clients and ensuring that we are always 'in place and in space' when the client is speaking is being able to actively listen to a prospect or client.

Prospects or clients who we facilitate through effective questions and quality listening always engage more willingly and create faster rapport with us.

The following six steps outline some of the things to be aware of when conducting client meetings and will immediately help to improve the quality of those client meetings.

L stands for LOOK and Look Interested:

When working with a client it is important that we maintain good eye contact with the client at all times. Good eye contact indicates that we are expressing an interest in the client and in his or her concerns.

Poor eye contact stems from not focusing our attention on the client's face or perhaps staring *too* intently at their features! There is a fine line between paying close and interested attention and seeming confrontational.

Looking at the client's face also allows us to pick up the unconscious facial signals that indicate the client's interest or lack of interest in what we are saying.

If, for example, we notice that the client is going glassy-eyed we can safely assume that they are losing interest – hence we may require greater flexibility in our means of communication with them. Less talking and more questions perhaps? Sketching it out on paper, getting the client more involved in the meeting?

Some clients prefer verbal communication while others prefer engaging through written communication. By bringing both into your presentation you will capture the full attention of any client.

For those of us uncomfortable with eye-contact, and many of us are, it's useful to remember to use what is known as the "business triangle of vision" that we covered in an earlier chapter.

This inverted triangular space extends from across the eyebrows down to the tip of the chin. When we direct our attention anywhere inside this area we make the client feel that we are completely engaging with them, while removing the discomfort we might feel by focusing our attention on their eyeballs!

An additional benefit to being able to look at the client directly and having them feel really engaged with us, is the fact that by our feeling more comfortable with the communication, so do they.

I stands for IDENTIFY the Issues:

People are interested in what interests them, so find out what that is. The best means of doing that is to ask a very simple question – *"what's MOST important to you about..?"*

This question helps us to identify the values upon which a person makes their decisions. Usually we would want to identify at least 3-4 values, and then identify the order in which they are most important.

Values are an important part of how people make their decisions. By identifying what they are, we are better positioned to influence those same decisions.

Finding out what issues concern our clients most is a guaranteed way of gaining their interest and their attention, and how our services can resolve their needs and wants for them.

S stands for SINCERITY:

We know when someone is being insincere with us don't we? Is it something that's bound to win our trust? So why would our clients be any different? We are all somebody's client.

Never promise things we can't deliver on. Always deliver a little more than is expected. Respect our client as we would ourselves and ensure that above all else, our dealings with our clients are based on the highest sense of integrity.

Relationships built on sincerity and integrity will last. It is on these relationships that our business future is secured.

T stands for TEST Your Understanding of what the client is saying:
Too often we can make errors in our suggestions, because we failed to question the client sufficiently around the specifics of their needs, or because we made an assumption.

It's OK to ask questions for clarification around what the client is most concerned about, it's not OK to assume we know the client's needs, as every client is different.

After all, we want to provide the best solution possible don't we? The best way of doing that is to question for a clearer understanding of the needs of each client in turn.

A simple question that one can ask when seeking clarification is the Exploratory or "How do you mean?" question. This question encourages the client to reflect on their statement and then repeat it back to us in a more coherent way, often allowing them to furnish us with information that may have been left out of the earlier answer.

E stands for ENTHUSIASM:
There is no substitute for being sincerely enthusiastic about providing a solution to our client's needs.

No matter how long in the tooth we might be in business, enthusiasm, that expression of a "can do" attitude when meeting with the client - has a magical effect.

Enthusiasm is infectious. It portrays a willingness to serve and to do our best in the process. It is an excellent persuasive tool in the process of reaching agreement with our client. In a service or consulting industry it is invaluable.

It's also worth noting that the last four letters of Enthusiasm – I.A.S.M – stand for *'I Am Sold Myself!'* If we bring what we love to our prospects and clients how hard can it be to get them to love it too?

N stands for NODS, NOISES and NOTES:
By feeding back to the client our understanding, agreement and interest in what they are saying through unconscious body language such as short verbal comments and nods, we communicate to the client that we are pacing their conversation and are maintaining interest in what concerns them.

By communicating only through nods and noises we are giving the client permission to keep talking, thus gathering further information around a specific topic, until it's time for us to again control the conversation through asking a relevant question.

Notes are invaluable in meetings. Do not expect to remember it all.

Keep notes discreetly, keeping them short to ensure maximum eye contact and direct interaction with the client, and remember that it's polite to ask if it's OK to take notes during the meeting.

So next time you are meeting with a client, try to remember the value in having the client do the talking. In the modern world people seldom get a chance to just talk and people are always impressed by people who are impressed by them.

So, if you want to improve your client influence significantly in the future, just L.I.S.T.E.N.

Coming up in our next chapter – how to overcome and even learn to love client objections.

Chapter 11: Learning to Love Objections

Objections are a normal factor of business so now let's explore why we, as High Trust Advisers, should *actively seek them out* rather than avoid them.

One of the greatest concerns that all novice or even experienced business advisers and relationship managers have, other than having to ask the client to close the deal, is facing objections to their business relationship.

However, some of the following points might help us to change our views on having to face objections to our proposals and so start to see how valuable and necessary they are in the business process.

Objections can act as guides as to how far along the client relationship we are, how well we are doing with the presentation, the level of buy-in from the prospect, and how close we are to closing the proposal.

Yet objections can occur for any number of reasons. Perhaps we haven't been listening actively for example and so missed a key piece of information or failed to ask the right kinds of question to clarify a client's response.

Or perhaps we have not addressed the objection sufficiently and there is a significant degree of ambiguity or lack of clarity in the mind of the client.

We might even be attempting to communicate our information in a way that is the complete opposite of the client's preferred style of communication. (See Chapter 9 Selling in Colour).

Personally, when objections are genuine (and not just being used to block or impede the presentation or to make the prospect look good to his/her peers), I *love* business objections and there are a number of reasons why:

1. We Often Confuse an 'Objection' With a 'Rejection'.

I've started to get worried about my father's past history as he's always very fond of quoting the Mafia! One of his favourite sayings is *'It's nothing personal – just business."*

Well business objections as just that, nothing personal, just business.

Remember that a prospect is not rejecting **us** they are simply objecting to the **business proposition**. The prospect does not **know** us, in fact, they know little or nothing about us so how can they be rejecting us personally?

What they are *really* objecting to is the lack of understanding they have about how the product or service that we are presenting brings any value to them.

What they're really saying is that they want more information.

2. In Business 'No' Seldom Means 'No - Forever' Just 'No - For Now'.

Too many people give up on a sale or a proposal when the prospect gives us the first 'No'.

But I'm going to ask you *not to stop* at the first 'No'. When a prospect says 'No' they often have some deeper reason below it, what we really need to do is to probe deeper into the real reason for the 'No'.

Find out if the timing is right, is this the right decision maker, have you the right service offering for them, do they have the budgets or do they not, do they understand what we're actually proposing.

Find out why they said 'No' in the first place and it may allow us to position the business proposition again at a later date in a more pertinent way.

A great question when a prospect says 'No' is *'How do you mean?'* – it encourages them to explain further or *'May I ask you why?'*

Never be afraid to ask the prospect to justify their response. It may just help you to find out the real motivation and then adapt your presentation accordingly.

3. Objections are Better than Indifference.

I can work with an objection because I can probe it or I can change the way I'm communicating. If they're objecting to what I'm presenting, then at least *they are engaged in the process* and trying to understand what it is we are proposing.

They are looking for more information or clarity or a reason to buy.

What I can't sell to is *indifference* – where someone has zero interest in what I'm proposing.

This can only occur if we got our prospecting criteria wrong in the first place and we are talking to the wrong person.

Alternatively, it may be happening because I have committed some error that I'm not aware of that has caused them some degree of annoyance, or has broken rapport and hence created passive resistance to me or the proposal.

Either way, it's time to move on. 'Selling' is about service, it's not about trying to ram what we have down their throats – that was the old days.

The world is an abundant place and it's so much easier to sell to people who have a need for our wares. Retreat, re-group and re-target and find the people who want what we have.

4. Maybe We're Not Communicating in Their Language.

Different people communicate and process information in different ways - as outlined in Chapter 9 Selling in Colour.

Some are *visual* so they like pictures and graphs (Red Warriors). They process information through pictures so they need to see brochures or graphs or models.

Some people are *auditory* (Yellow Entertainers) or do their mental processing through sound. As a result, they like to chat and verbalise things with others and require personal interaction and the chance to vocalise.

Other prospects are '*feeling*' (Green Healers) and like time to reflect and 'get a feel' for the product or service. They might want to handle or touch it or be assured that others are already using it successfully and speak well of it.

Finally, some people are *analytical* (Blue Mystics) and prefer to get their information in written form in advance of any sales meeting so that they have the time to reflect on the proposition and do not want to be forced into making a decision.

Just as an example I was working a few years ago with a software company in Dallas, Texas.

By just taking the time to learn about the personality (processing) types that they sold to (bankers – predominantly Blue) and the personality style of their business development team (predominantly Red-Yellow), they learned to move from an auditory style to an analytical style and so increase their call to appointment ratio by almost a factor of ten.

They increased their call to meeting ratio from 4 appointments in every 100 calls to 38 appointments in every 100 calls. Now that's progress.

To be sure that we get our point across effectively we must make sure that we **use verbal, visual and written styles** to make the most effective presentation.

5. Handle Objections with 'Specifically'

Ambiguity or lack of clarity will kill a business proposal so make sure that we get the *facts* and not general responses or assumptions.

If a prospect makes a statement or creates an objection we can often get a great deal of clarity around it, and so deal with it, if we probe using the six 'open' questions (How, What, Where , Why, When and Who) and the word **Specifically**.

How **Specifically**, When **Specifically**, Who **Specifically** and so on can have the prospect dissect their objections and allow us to find a way through the objection and carry on with the business process.

6. Each Objection is a Step Closer to the Prize

Every objection successfully met and dealt with is a step closer to closing the business. Not only that but objections can be turned around and turned into buying reasons.

'You don't have it in blue' - 'If I could get it for you in blue would you be interested in going ahead?'

'I don't have the budget' - 'If we could bill you next quarter could we look at proceeding?'

Objections can be a tremendous help in calibrating where we are in the business process.

Because they indicate that the prospect is engaging with us and exhibiting a degree of interest, they are far better than having to handle indifference.

Each objection successfully handled is a step closer to closing the deal, so learn to welcome them and use them as valuable tools in creating even greater business success by sustaining and monetising the lifetime value of the client.

In the next chapter we explore a key skill of any business adviser or relationship manager – presenting for profit.

Chapter 12: Presenting for Profit

A key part of any business relationship is when we get the opportunity to present our solution or service.

Finally the opportunity to pitch has arrived, and here is where we can fail disastrously or emerge victorious from the time and effort we have invested in initiating, nurturing and deepening our relationship with the client.

Even if the audience are existing clients or our colleagues – perhaps key business stakeholders - how we are seen to present is a key competency of being a High Trust Adviser.

I want to highlight some key factors that heighten the power of a presentation and, most importantly, the amount of 'take home' that the audience (whoever they are) get from the presentation.

The quality and number of these 'take homes' will ensure that our presentation is both memorable – and profitable.

The **WHW** Structure:
The structure of a presentation is critical and in many cases it is the one area where presentations can go badly wrong right from the start.

We live in a world where the attention span of an audience has become significantly reduced for things that do not grab their interest from the start.

Now whether we blame YouTube, computer gaming, smart phones or the ease of 'channel surfing' one thing is certain – the attention span of the modern audience has become very short for things that do not interest them.

Today an audience's attention is won or lost in the first few minutes of the presentation – so we need to capture their attention from the very start.

So if that is the case why do people persist in using an outmoded presentation structure?

Why is it that I still see presentations that start with the old traditional approach of *Why* ...we are such a great company to do business with....*How* ...we are so great at what we do.....and *What* (finally) ...we can do for you and the result of this traditional presentation structure (especially with Red Warrior decision-makers)?

Using this traditional structure the audience has already tuned-out so that by the time you get to the value proposition the decision-makers are no longer engaged.

This traditional presentation structure needs to be *inverted* – away from the traditional Why, How and What to **What, How and Why** instead.

We should start by changing our presentation to leading with the **What** ...we can do for you. Here is where we state right from the start the huge benefits we bring to them.

State clearly and distinctly for the audience what *specifically* we can do for *them*, what they will have when they work with us – and use our 'points of compelling relevance' – so that the language is simple, concise, meaningful and present-tense.

In addition, if we have done our research correctly, we can place each PCR against a specific client value that we have identified and sequenced in earlier meetings using our questioning skills.

Think what a powerful impact that can make.

Now we've just switched on the audience to the value and benefits in clear simple language that they will get from using our services or products (and we have aligned those benefits with their key decision-making values) - right from the very first words that we use in the presentation.

Now the question in the audience's mind is **How** can we deliver this? They are interested, engaged and seeking answers. They want to know.

Instead of their attention having been lost they are actively listening, filling in the blanks, searching for ways in which their issues can be resolved. They are now with us.

Finally the audience will ask **Why** they should use us as providers and here is where we establish our credibility, experience and resources. This is the final piece of the journey that the audience has willingly taken with us and where they become convinced of the value of our solution.

So we should move from the traditional structure of Why, How and What to the more effective and logical structure of **What, How and Why** and see our presentation impact soar.

In addition I urge people to stop thinking about presentations in the traditional formal manner. People want to be connected, involved and engaged so think about how we structure a *dialogue* with the audience and not just a *monologue*.

Think about a *conversation* and not a *presentation* and everything will run smoothly.

Stories

Remember as a child the power of the phrase 'Once Upon a Time'...?

It instantly prepared us for story time - for adventures and magic and tales of far away and mythical lands – dropping us into a powerfully suggestible trance.

Stories are how humanity has shared information and experience from the very first days. Note the longevity of mythological stories, and how even today we perk up when someone has news or a bit of gossip....

Stories in presentations are very powerful and we should craft stories that can serve as metaphors or platforms for our key business points.

Some reasons for why stories are powerful business presentation tools are as follows:

1. There is very little resistance to stories – people do not see themselves as being 'pitched at' or 'sold to' when stories are used to illustrate points, so their normal resistance and scepticism is lowered.

2. The audience associates with the characters in a story – taking the position and the viewpoint of the key person and living their experiences in the story. This can be a powerful suggestive tool encouraging people to take the same decisions or actions as the story's central character.

3. Stories don't have to be true – they just have to be *plausible*. Stories do not have to be dry case studies and they can be powerful means of suggesting things to an audience. Also, because they are stories, we can use them to position ideas in the mind of an audience without the necessity for exact logical proof. Simply being plausible, that something is possible, is enough to get the

message across and effect change in the mind of the audience.

4. Developing stories – either real case studies but converted into genuine stories rather than cold facts or stories that are simply made up to highlight a key point, allows us to powerfully influence any audience.

Self-Confidence:
Presenting to a live audience is seen by some people as an even greater fear than death itself. People will literally do anything to get out of having to make a presentation to a group.

I have seen how this fear can paralyse and render incapable otherwise intelligent and articulate people. Managing one's confidence is therefore important if one wishes to appear fluent, competent and professional.

First let me just say that it's OK to be nervous.

In fact it's a *good thing* because it means that we *care* about what it is we are going to say.

As someone once said *'it's fine to have butterflies in the stomach – as long as they are all flying in formation!'*. I always get nervous before a speech but it helps keep me sharp. So nerves can actually *help* a presenter.

The High Trust Adviser by Seán Weafer

Too many nerves are not good however and so we need to learn to manage our state prior to any presentation. So here are a few pointers that may help:

1. Live Rehearsal – helps fluency and importantly timing. (By the way please finish a presentation by when you say you will. Two minutes before time and they love us, two minutes after the time and they are looking for a way out).

   Repetition is internalisation, the more often we do it in rehearsal the more likely it is to be successful. As they say in martial arts - the more we sweat in training, the less we bleed in battle.

2. Mental Rehearsal - running a successful outcome to the presentation over and over in our mind is a powerful means of managing personal state, and used extensively by athletes.

   The mind cannot tell the difference between a real and imagined memory so the more often we rehearse things in our mind the more the mind believes that this is something that we do every day.

   Picture the audience being interested, engaged and giving us a powerfully positive reception to our presentation. This helps reduce the fear of the event because the mind assumes that this is a familiar thing for us and not something being done for the first time.

3. Put something relevant about ourselves into the opening of a presentation.

At the very start of the presentation, where it is appropriate, we should take the opportunity to introduce ourselves with something that connects with the audience.

There are two benefits to this –

1. It allows us to talk about the one thing no-one can question us on - ourselves. We are the sole expert on ourselves and this can help us start to relax into the presentation

2. It allows us to start to build a relationship with the audience by sharing something in our introduction that connects with them.

4. Finally, remember our authority. We are in the room with the expectation of the audience that we are an expert in the subject and content of our presentation. If we have rehearsed and prepared then there is no reason why we cannot deliver on that expectation every time.

When it comes to confidence in a presentation the difference between fear and fluency - is passion and practice.

Engaging the Audience

Managing an audience is critical to a successful presentation. So let's look at a few pointers that can help with this area.

The Light House:

Keeping an audience's attention involves maintaining good eye contact. That means that we need to 'sweep' the audience with our eyes on a regular basis – just like a lighthouse.

This ensures that the audience sees that we are engaged, we continue to assess audience reaction to our points and keep the audience itself on their toes and awake!

This is particularly important when we are using a slide presentation or a flipchart.

There can be a tendency to read the screen or turn away from the audience which can be disastrous – because breaking eye contact with them can lose us their attention.

To minimise this happening, we should have a copy of the presentation in front of us, where we can glance at it without having to turn away from the audience. Sometimes it's possible to have another screen positioned in front of us that matches what is being shown on the main screen.

Questions:

We have already looked in great detail at the power of questions and suggestions, and the advanced questioning skills that we can bring to bear on a prospect or client, as a means of managing a meeting.

But questions can also be used in presentations to ensure that the audience is equally engaged in the presentation.

After all, as I said at the start of this chapter, where does it say that all presentations should be about us having a monologue (one way communication) with the audience when a dialogue (two-way communication) is so much more powerful and engaging?

The challenge can sometimes be in handling the audiences questions however and so here are a couple of ideas about how handle them professional and fluently.

1. The Car Park

    Sometimes time constraints on a presentation can reduce the time to adequately deal with questions. So one way to ensure that we have the time to complete our presentation and deal with questions is to use what's termed the Car Park.

    Agree with the audience from the start - to ensure that we finish on time – that we will not answer questions during the presentation. However we will happily take questions from the floor as they arise and note them on a flipchart.

Once we have delivered the presentation then the last thing that we do is turn to the flipchart where we have written down the audiences questions.

As we move down the list of questions, answering with each one of them in turn, we may then find that a number of the questions have already been dealt with during the presentation.

Other questions will not have been dealt with, and so we use the opportunity there and then to answer those questions.

As we answer each question we use a marker to place a big 'tick' or 'correct' sign beside each answered question.

By leaving this on display, when we bring the session to an end, the audience (as they depart) can see that every question has been answered and every question is 'correct' and has been resolved.

This can be a powerful visual anchor for an audience to have at the end of any presentation.

2. Difficult Questions

   When faced with difficult questions from the audience how we handle them will be a clear indicator as to our professionalism as a High Trust Adviser.

   Firstly if we do not know the answer to the question then say so but we can then use it as an opportunity to compliment then questioner.

   We might say something like: '....that is an excellent question. To be honest I had not considered it but if you give me a little time I'll come back with the relevant answer'

   Then make sure we do, (with supporting documentation) and ensure that the rest of the audience knows that we have. Copy them for example on the email that responds to the question.

   Secondly, a question can sometimes be asked because the questioner wishes to assert their dominance to the group, or their knowledge, or to get attention or simply to throw us off balance.

   In such a case we can throw a difficult question back at someone. 'Interesting question. You seem to have given this some thought what are your ideas?'

Alternatively if the person has been consistently interrupting a presentation to score points we can sometimes ask them a difficult question and before they have time to respond say 'and while X are considering that let us move on with the presentation and we can then come back..' (of course we never do…!)

A variation on that is to ask the rest of the audience to comment with 'that is an interesting perspective. May I ask what the rest of the audience think?'

I've seen this question used to powerful effect on an audience. When asked, the audience itself rounded on the questioner and made their opinion felt as to what they thought about the constant interruption.

It is very important that we ourselves as the presenter do not engage in argument with any member of the audience. Doing so can only lose us key credibility and rapport with an audience.

These simple pointers can help add a professional, confident and effective edge to any presentation we make and ensure that our presentations are memorable, engaging and successful.

Chapter 13: Creating a Success Mindset

High trust advisers are success focused and understand that success is the *achievement of pre-defined goals*.

Therefore to achieve success it requires that we have clear written goals that map out our desires and the actions necessary to take them.

In the next two chapters we'll cover the psychology behind setting goals that work. We'll cover some of the key secrets of setting and achieving powerful new outcomes and we'll also cover the ways to make goal-setting a fantastic habit for mega-success, and how it can boost our personal motivation, to keep us going when others fall.

Nothing great was ever achieved without planning.

Imagine the planning it took to put Neil Armstrong on the moon and bring him and his crew back safely. It is just such planning and goal-setting that creates the future history of tomorrow.

It reminds me of a story I was once told about Christopher Columbus, the great explorer.

Surprisingly this was probably the least well-planned voyage of exploration ever undertaken by mankind. Why?

Well, because when Columbus set out he didn't know where he was going. When he got there, he didn't know where he was and when he got back...he didn't know where he'd been!

Caught up in the momentum of today's world few of us have the luxury of investing that sort of time and expense to achieve our aims in life. Yet we need clear goals to guarantee our chances of success, to 'future-proof' our businesses and careers.

Many successful businesses lay plans for the future, yet it constantly amazes me how few of the people charged with delivering business goals have actually set specific goals for their own performance.

Taking the time to understand clearly how to set and achieve goals can provide us all with 7 key benefits:

1. A clear direction in our lives and careers and a sense of adventure about its outcome.

2. A measure by which to benchmark the successes that we have along the way.

3. A boost in our self-confidence, as a result of our success and proof of our abilities.

4. A powerful means of coping with change and stress. By knowing in advance what we can do to adapt and succeed

despite the challenges that we face – we can cope with the stress of future uncertainty more effectively.

5. The ability to communicate our needs more effectively. Once we know clearly what we want and why we want it - then enlisting the aid of others through communicating our intention improves our success rate and again reduces our personal stress levels.

6. The ability to improve our strengths and overcome our weaknesses. Often by identifying our strengths and working towards them we overcome weaknesses by removing their impact, as they become less relevant to the action that we take to move forward.

7. A better quality of life. This can be assisted by all of the above benefits of deciding what the future *should* be instead of waiting for what life will throw at you. It is better to create one's future than it is to try and predict it.

Yet despite these obvious benefits, many business professionals still do one thing wonderfully well, we take the time to plan to fail, simply by failing to plan.

Check yourself against these reasons of why we often fail to plan our future success:

1. We Don't Understand the Importance of Setting Goals.
2. We Fear Failure and/or Rejection.

3. We Fear Success.
4. We Simply Don't Take the Time.
5. We Don't Know How to Set Goals - or Set Them Too High Initially and Get Discouraged from further action.
6. We Fail to Raise Our Personal Standards.
7. We Fail to Empower Our Goals by Using Our Subconscious Mind and Understanding Our Motivation.

Let's look at some of the main reasons of why we still fail to set specific outcomes for ourselves:

We Fear Failure/Rejection: We can consider both of these together because fear of failure is often closely linked to the fear of rejection.

Acceptance is the highest of human needs as we are essentially social creatures, so anything that threatens that is to be instinctively avoided.

However, if in protecting our sense of ourselves we let that same sense wither and die for want of taking a risk, where is the excitement in life's game? Where is the rebelliousness that brings life to the act of living?

Even failure is a process of learning. Every time we fail, we learn the next time to use a different approach.

For those of us who can swim, we had to swallow a lot of water before we achieved proficiency. Every time we sank our instinctive learning mechanism filed away the learning by which we could do it better the next time.

In the same way we learned to drive or ride a bicycle - by failing and by taking the learning from the failure until we built up a sufficient understanding of the process to do it right and then improve upon it.

Our brain analysed and applied it until we had 'hard wired' the new behaviours into our system, creating a habit or competency.

Success is often just such a gradual process. Few if any "overnight" successes have no history of failures from which years later their "overnight" success was born.

We should "dare to fail" and in the failing, find the learning that leads to a better understanding of the means of achieving our goal. Few rewards are earned without risk and those that are we seldom value.

Successful people know that life is not about being 'perfect' as some would have us believe. Life is about 'perfecting' where the journey requires us to fail, to learn from it, to be human, to forgive and to grow.

We Fear Success: It's strange to consider that we might actually fear success. But in fact, this is one of our greatest fears.

This is because success brings responsibility.

It creates standards that, once we create them, we have to continue to live up to.

Standards that then can be used to criticise us should we fail at some future, undefined date, to meet them.

It also brings a fear of the consequences that may occur after we have achieved our desired goals. If I achieve this goal, what would I lose? Who would I upset?

Have you ever heard someone say, "I'd LOVE to win a few million in the Lottery, you know three or maybe even four million.......but NOT twenty million, God no, that's ridiculous...that'd ruin your life!"

So we sometimes need to check the possible consequences of achieving our goals.

When setting a personal or professional goal it can be important to ask first 'what would I gain if I achieve this goal?' or 'what would I lose if I gain this goal?'

If the answer is in conflict with either our personal or professional values then the chances are that we could have a significant lack of motivation towards achieving this goal.

There is always a balance in successful outcomes which demands that a price be paid for our success. To be successful we often need to decide what that price will be and if we are prepared to pay it.

We Don't Take the Time: We can always find the time for something we really consider important can't we? Deciding goals is an unconscious process, something we do quite naturally every day. What makes the *difference* is in prioritising, clarifying and committing them to paper.

The relatively little time taken to invest in setting down goals can lead to far greater rewards, from far less effort. Self-discipline is the key. Make a start. Then it becomes surprisingly easy and even fun.

We Don't Know How to Set Goals Properly: In the first flush of each New Year we set resolutions which last as long as the season.

Often we set our resolutions (or goals) too high, setting ourselves up for failure through overreaching ourselves. This then often discourages us from further endeavours.

It's understandable – for when were we ever shown how to create a manual for our life or our business?

We certainly were never born with one. Perhaps we may have had to scramble through life or career up to now. But now we have the power to change that, now we have the power to choose our destinies and make them real through focused action.

We Fail to Raise Our Personal or Professional Standards:
As long as we expect little of ourselves we will get just that - little.

Our future can be dictated not by what has gone before, but by the decisions that we make in the present. In deciding a future we need to raise our standards and our expectations of ourselves and of those around us.

It is the nature of life that if we are not learning and growing, then we are stagnating. We get exactly what the mind expects. Positive thinking is thinking about what you want. Instead, most of us focus our minds on what we don't want. As a result, we get exactly what we *don't* want to happen.

Our expectations should always exceed our experiences.

Goals fill our psycho-computer with the programming necessary to create the desired behaviour for our success – and expectations drive behaviours.

We Fail to Empower Goals With Our Subconscious:
Our subconscious mind represents a largely unknown portion of our total mental power. Success is guaranteed when we

learn to access it for our goals and begin the process of *synchronicity*.

Synchronicity is the means whereby we become aware of attracting people or events into our lives by deciding on a goal. It's almost as if we send out an unconscious signal that feeds back the information that we need to be successful in our efforts.

Focusing on something raises our awareness of possibilities and opens opportunities.

As a simple example, have you ever considered buying a car, and then when you bought it (invested value in it) *that* was when you noticed just how many of that particular type of car there are actually on the roads - you just never noticed before, until you *focused* on it.

Having considered the importance of our goals, now let's consider the foundations of how power-goals can be set and mega-achievement created.

There are 5 foundations to achievable outcomes or successful goals.

The first is **VISION**. Vision is the capacity to see beyond where we are in the present and imagine a future that is all that it can be. This *encourages* us to raise our standards and gives us the capability to start to overcome the self-limiting beliefs which we all harbour.

Often we can obstruct this creative faculty within us. We are conditioned to believe that all the goals we set should be realistic and achievable.

While most goals certainly need to be achievable to maintain our motivation, when *all* our goals are based entirely on our experiences and beliefs about ourselves to-date, our ability to leap to a new plateaux of performance is greatly limited. Sometimes it pays to "take the road less travelled".

The great leaders through time – all of them rebels willing to look beyond the boundaries of convention - have always been inspired by visions of greater glories or worlds that have yet to be. For good or ill it is precisely because of those visions that the world progressed.

Inspiration is motivation.

The second is **DESIRE**. A want is stronger than a wish. We often achieve what we want but seldom what we wish for.

Desire takes place when we associate more pleasure than pain with the outcome. Therefore we should set goals only for what we really desire.

Only goals that are meaningful to us will be fuelled by the power of desire. Desire is the inner fire that sets our futures alight.

Setting goals simply because they appear impressive to others wastes time. Setting goals because they return a real and tangible benefit for us creates the motivation we need to move toward our specified outcomes.

The third foundation is **RESPONSIBILITY**. Responsibility is something that has fallen out of fashion in the present. Yet it is something that is essential to success.

It is essential to achieving our outcomes in the ever faster pacing world of today and tomorrow. We must hold ourselves accountable for our actions and decisions.

Reaching for goals involves challenge. By taking responsibility for the way in which we meet those challenges, by being honest with ourselves, we can apply the flexibility necessary to meet those challenges and achieve our objectives.

The secret to having more control over our careers and lives is simple. TAKE MORE RESPONSIBILITY.

The fourth is **COMMITMENT**. Goals without personal commitment are just wasted effort.

We must begin a thing and learn to accept our failures, for failures there may be, as *learning* rather than as setbacks.

Our level of commitment is determined by the amount of gain or pleasure we subscribe to the achievement of our goals. Commitment also means that we take those first steps to achievement, which can often prove the hardest.

But to overcome the inertia which is at first associated with great undertakings - *simply begin.*

In time, if we have set our goals correctly, the successes of the smaller goals will drive us forward to successfully reach our overall outcome.

Commitment requires the steel of self-discipline - the ability to see our focus and our desires through to their fulfilment.

The fifth foundation is **HONEST EVALUATION**.

There's a saying that says that "you can lie to everybody else, but always be true to yourself."

We must be prepared to tell ourselves the "hard stuff" about whether we are really putting in the effort to make things happen. We need to monitor ourselves regularly about our level of commitment and the tasks achieved to-date.

This has the added bonus of improving our flexibility to decide new plans of action where circumstances merit, to ensure we stay on track, until we reach our goal.

The most important thing about goals is the ability to make them a part of our everyday thinking. Make them a habit for ourselves so that *every day* we take action towards their achievement and our satisfaction.

One of the ways of creating a habit or *an unconscious repetitive response* is to create goals in a manner that they are most easily accepted by the powerhouse of our unconscious mind.

Our unconscious (or subconscious) mind has a number of important points about which all successful goal-setters should be aware.

1. The unconscious mind is designed to protect and heal the body.

The unconscious mind's prime directive is to protect and heal the body - even if that means making us sick sometimes. For example if excessive stress is wearing us down, the unconscious can make us sick in order to take the much needed rest that the body needs.

Take athletes who are coping badly with the pressure of an important game, it is amazing how many ankles get sprained, or illnesses set-in prior to the game. Take a performer or someone who develops stage fright, how many develop laryngitis or tonsillitis before a show. In this case, for our unconscious mind, illness is better than facing the fear of what they are expected to do.

Therefore successful planning should take into consideration all areas of our life and career in order to ensure that balance and harmony is maintained and that we can enjoy the fruits of our achievement.

There should be an ecological side to our planning, not in the sense of the natural environment of the planet, but in an understanding of the *consequences* of the goals we set.

2. The unconscious mind loves priority, association and specificity.

The unconscious mind reacts better when things have a sense of urgency about them, therefore goals should be prioritised in order of importance - first things first.

It also loves association or linkages, so ideally similar or supporting goals should be grouped together. This helps our unconscious focus more effectively on them. It encourages further links between the goals as the creative and intuitive side of the unconscious goes to work on making life that much easier for itself, by often providing unique new ways to achieve goals.

The unconscious mind is lazy and takes the easy way out wherever possible. Therefore goals should be as specific as possible.

It's not enough to say I want to make more money - walking down the street and finding a coin fulfils that requirement as far as the unconscious is concerned. Be specific, HOW MUCH MONEY SPECIFICALLY...do I want.

Make it work for you and never settle for less than that.

The remarkable thing about our unconscious mind is that it will move heaven and earth to ensure that what is happening in our *external* world, is a direct reflection of our *internal* world and our *internal* world is a direct reflection of the expectations that we create through setting power goals.

For example, can you remember how the world often seems a terrible place when things aren't going too well and yet how wonderful it appears and how lucky you seem to be when you're feeling GREAT!

Change your mind and you can change your world. When training top sales people and account managers I often teach them that attitude is 80% of a sale. In other words, what they expect from the client is often what they will get from the relationship.

3. The subconscious mind holds most of our mental energy.

The subconscious mind is often likened to the 90% of iceberg that lies beneath the surface of the water. It is silent, deep and powerful. I also like to think it is more like the engine room of a ship. It doesn't see where the ship is bound, that's the job of the captain on the bridge (the conscious mind).

But it provides the power to drive the ship across the wild and wide seas of life. The ship is powerless and directionless until the conscious and subconscious minds are working in harmony - direction and motivation.

4. It accepts simple, present-tense, instructions.

The subconscious recognises no past or future. Only the present exists in its world. Every day is today.

Therefore all instructions to it, such as goals, should be structured that way. After all, it drives our physical health and well-being. What if it instructed your heart to beat in thirty minutes time or that the next time you drew a breath would be next week?

How immediately and in what tense do you think it needs to receive it's instructions about our *other* needs?

Write your goals using the five P's:

Positive such that the goal or need is stated in a positive sense

Present Tense as explained above, so that it impacts more urgently on our subconscious mind

Personal again to help to drive the unconscious which recognises only itself

Passionate using emotive words to drive the subconscious which responds to strong emotions

Particular or exactly stated so that the unconscious knows exactly what it must do

Intention is very important when setting goals - to ensure the best results start goals by writing "I want to " it is a much more powerful statement of intent that I wish, I would, I hope etc.

5. The unconscious mind cannot tell the difference between real and imagined memories.

Can you remember a time when you recounted an event that had happened to you, only to make yourself look better or seem to have played a larger part than actually occurred, let's say you embellished the story of the event *just a little* when re-telling the event later to some friends.

Then you told the story again and again and again and then you forgot about it.....until someone asked you to tell the story again, but 6 months later. Only now you couldn't remember what had *actually* happened, and what you had added, it was *all* real to you.

Repetition had created a reality composed of truth and half-truth.

When working with the unconscious things only have to be *plausible* to be accepted as fact. In effect, we can re-create our past histories leaving our failures behind and re-programming only the experiences of success into our future behaviours.

Clinical hypnosis techniques make use of this fact when helping people safely re-visit old and emotional memories and handle the emotions surrounding them. A person can re-live the event in a safe way, take the learning and cope with the grief or fear associated with the event, which leads to a subsequent improvement in the person's behaviour and health.

6. It processes through vivid pictures and strong emotions - mental rehearsal.

Our unconscious psycho-computer is programmed through clear, vivid pictures and with strong emotion.

That is why we must *create a pictorial representation* of our future goal - the more colourful the image the better. In fact, if we add *sound, movement, brightness, clarity, even smells* to the future picture, then the *more* real it becomes to our "movie of the mind".

Where possible we should include ourselves in some way in the picture we create. This communicates to our unconscious that *this* is its target.

If we experience the future as if we have it, the unconscious will assume that we have achieved our goal already and will not focus on the objective. For the record, this is known as dissociated and associated mental rehearsal but more of this later.

Vivid emotion comes from the fact that our goal should be meaningful to us. The unconscious is the seat of our emotions and through them we can stimulate and communicate with it.

However you imagine the goal is perfectly OK, some people will be more colourful or accurate or clear than others. However you imagine the image is the right way for you. Practice will help.

In the unconscious there is no such thing as doing it the wrong way, once a positive intent or meaning is attached to the thought.

Within us all is the power to change worlds. It is in the imagination that the empires of the past were first raised and within the fires of the imagination that the dreams of the future are born.

Learning to use that imagination to empower your goals is a valuable skill. The subconscious mind is the seat of our emotions and provides the desire and energy to motivate us to achieve our intended objectives.

The High Trust Adviser by Seán Weafer

We communicate with our unconscious through the use of vividly imagined scenarios or pictures and emotions. It is important that while we create these pictures in our minds we also create the imagined sounds, tastes, smells, touches and feelings that would accompany the experience.

In effect, imagine that we can create a theatre in our mind and that we can create, as the director of our own life-movie, any scene that we choose.

If we then invest that scene with the feelings, sounds, tastes, smells etc. we are, in effect, programming our mental computer to generate the behaviour that will lead us to our goal.

What we are doing through such programming is creating expectations, which in turn create new 'engrams' or neural patterns in our brain, such that our behaviour would be modified to be more in line with our expected goal.

There are two ways in which the mind can picture the required successful outcome. The first is in an ASSOCIATED manner and the second a DISSOCIATED manner.

The manner and order that we chose to view the outcome in is very important.

Stage 1 - ASSOCIATED:

When viewing the goal outcome in this manner we are experiencing the goal as if we are physically viewing it through our own eyes. We are also experiencing the imagined senses of feelings, touch, tastes, sounds etc. as if we are physically present.

In this situation we cannot 'see' ourselves in the film-scene of the outcome's picture because we are actually imagining the experience of what it feels like to have accomplished the goal.

This is important as a first step once we have clearly identified our goal as it gives our unconscious mind an experience of what it would be like to have achieved the goal. This creates desire, intention and motivation within our subconscious.

Try this exercise: Imagine yourself walking up to your dream car. Now see if you can just notice your hands and your feet as you reach out and touch the hood.

Notice the colour of the car, feel the coolness of the metal under your touch. Now reach back and take the door handle and open the door. Smell that fresh new car smell as you slide yourself into the car seat and feel the comfort of it. Reach out and notice your hands closing firmly around the driving wheel. Take a firm grip. Notice how the surface feels, notice the instrument lay-out.

Close the door and hear the heavy 'thunk' as the door seals out the sounds outside of the car. Now reach down and turn the car ignition. Hear that sound?

Welcome back. Did you enjoy that?

However, from a mental programming point of view it is absolutely vital that we then carry out stage two.

Stage 2 - DISSOCIATED

This stage is where we pretend to jump-out of our body and sit in a cinema seat to enjoy the movie of us living the goal. In this circumstance we are IN the picture - so we are actually seeing ourselves in the scene.

It is essential to do this for, if we recall that the unconscious cannot tell the difference between an imagined and real experience, if we remained viewing the goal in an associated state it would simply assume that we had accomplished our goal and therefore would not provide the energy necessary to reach the goal in real terms.

Now, imagine yourself walking up to the car. See yourself reaching out and laying your hand on the hood of the car. Now see yourself reaching back and opening the car door and sitting inside. Notice yourself in the car looking around and then reaching down to turn on the engine. Now imagine yourself just driving off in your dream car.

By jumping-out of the picture and seeing ourselves within the film scene we are now giving the unconscious a message - "Look that's what I want, you know what it feels like to have it, wouldn't it be great to have it again?"

This is the key principle behind the use of mental rehearsal to empower goals, helps get 'our brain in the game' and drive our motivation to succeed.

In the next chapter I'll explain how great professionals commit to and achieve powerful performance goals.

Chapter 14: Practical Performance Goals

Now let's look at the practical work required to create effective performance goals.

Keys to Success

What follows are the six key steps to successful goal accomplishment.

1. Always Write Down Your Goals.

The act of writing down our goals is the magic formula that externalises what up to now have been mere mental wishes, and this simple act creates mental *intention*. It is the first act of commitment in what then becomes a process of success.

Writing down our goals creates a benchmark which can be used to measure our growing success, our need to re-appraise, to re-focus and to re-commit where necessary.

It is the first act in the process of creating our successful futures. It is an absolute requirement in the art and science of success and determines the measure of the successes to follow.

2. Space Your Goals Over Ninety-Day Periods.

The timing of goals is crucial. There should be enough time to allow things to occur. As a rule, goals should be worked over a

3-6 month period (short term), 6-12 month period (medium term) and 1-3 year years (long term).

Goals *over* 3 years tend to fall into the category of life-goals. They are ideal scenarios which the shorter timed goals are creating the foundations for.

For ease of action the 6-12 week cycle is often the most efficient for business purposes. This is the time scale I use with my coaching clients and I see powerful goals achieved in just twelve short weeks through clarity, intention, action and accountability.

3. Review Your Goals Regularly - Repetition Makes It Work

Once written, goals need to be regularly re-visited. This keeps them firmly in our minds and keeps us on the fast track to success and achievement.

It also brings in the magic of repetition. By repetition we set up new neural pathways in our minds, pathways which alter our behaviour and create new habits of success. Remember your multiplication tables....."one by two is two, two by two is four"......a simple demonstration of the power of repetition all these years later.

4. Where Possible Choose a Goal-Partner.

Often even with the best of intentions we seldom perform at our optimum by ourselves. We can benefit greatly from someone external to ourselves to hold us accountable to ourselves, someone that we can share our goals with. This could be a professional coach or a master mind group – a small group of selected people with whom we work with to accomplish our goals and help them to accomplish theirs.

Excellence is often a matter of partnership.

5. Break All Large Goals Down Into Sub-Goals or Activities.

Even the largest of goals can be achieved if we "task" them or break them down into smaller pieces - even the biggest challenges can be faced when broken into smaller pieces.

The goals can be broken into tasks or actions which can then be monitored on a weekly basis. Actions keep you on-track towards your goals on a weekly and even daily schedule.

The added advantage of tasking goals is that our subconscious *loves* success.

If we are being successful at the smaller things it provides more personal energy and *more* motivation to face the next challenge and the next and so on. Pretty soon, we've accomplished our largest objectives.

6. Stay Flexible

Success requires flexibility of approach.

Water travelling from a mountain spring to its ultimate goal of the sea is seldom stopped by rock. It finds a way. Over, around, under or eventually through erosion it overcomes all obstacles, refusing to contemplate failure or denial of its objective.

Setting out to create personal future history will create obstacles for us - after all, we have to prove we are worthy of the goal and take the learning from the process. Remember to think of the water flowing to the sea - cool, fluid and unstoppable.

The S.M.A.R.T. Model

The SMART model is an excellent format in common use for structuring goals and is based on the idea of goals being drafted as follows:

S for Specific and Simple: The unconscious mind responds to instructions that are highly specific and simply given.

Just as one would write a line of programming code for computer software - keep it simple, keep it clean, keep it exact. Our goals should be simply stated and highly specific as regards the positive outcome we require from them. This is the beginning of the spells of succeeding magically.

M for Measurable and Meaningful: There has to be a means of monitoring our success with the goal and it has to be of value to us - hence it needs to be meaningful.

Only something that inspires excitement and *passion within us* can carry us forward to overcome our natural resistance to change, to effect an improvement of our circumstances.

A for As If Now & Achievable: Goals *always* need to be expressed in the present tense in *order to tap the help of* our unconscious energies.

Our unconscious mind cannot recognise a past or a future - *only actions in the present tense* - hence our goals should be stated in the present.

One of the best ways of phrasing goals with positive and present intent is to start with the words "I want to ..."

Goals need to be achievable. There's little point to setting goals that are patently out of our reach. We need to have the resources necessary or can eventually access the resources necessary in time to make our goals achievable ones.

R is for Realistic & Responsible: Goals should generally be within the bounds of our ability - although this should not be an excuse for not raising our standards to improve our capabilities.

For example, it would be unrealistic for most of us ordinary mortals to expect that we could survive on Mount Everest's peak in just a bathing suit.

The secret of life is this – **personal responsibility is the key to personal power.**

The more responsibility we take for our lives, the more control we have within it. Our goals affect others, we need to remember that when setting our outcomes.

T is for Time Bound and Towards: Set a deadline. When did we study the hardest for exams? (..if you were a student like me then usually just the night before the exam!)

We all need a little stress to get us motivated. Without a deadline goals are just unfulfilled dreams.

So, set a date and stick to it.

In the field of Neuro Linguistic Programming (NLP) there is the study of values and how they affect our beliefs. They are what attract and repel us, they guide our behaviours. They have two directions - *Towards,* which is the positive aspect and *Away From*, which is the negative aspect.

An example of a Positive Towards goal might be "to be rich" - if asked why, we might reply "to care for me and my family". That is a *'Towards'* goal as it strengthens and helps us and is motivated by care for ourselves and those close to us.

An example of a negative '*Away From*' goal might also be "to be rich" - however, if asked why, we might reply "so I won't be poor".

The need is to move away from a negative state. While this may have short-term motivation benefits, it seldom lasts for the long-term and can create stress and encourage frustration, as we find the goal harder to achieve. In fact our performance and motivation often disappear the further away we get from the negative state we wanted to 'move away' from.

Lastly, all goals should have some form of mental inner representation, a picture of what it would be like to actually have the goal accomplished. This is important as a tool for programming the unconscious and releasing the power of the mind. We often call this "mental rehearsal" when we apply it to athletes and we will discuss this in more detail in the last message.

The SMART goal sheet is the model to use when setting your goals for a successful future.

A good way to first identify goals would be to ask ourselves the following questions:

1. What is the *greatest* challenge facing me right now or what one thing could I do such that if I do it – it would affect the greatest amount of change for me?

2. What sort of things would I LOVE to be doing in the job right now?

The first question helps us identify the most important thing that needs doing, while the second question helps us identify those things that can massively enhance our performance.

Make a list from the answers to these questions and then choose the first goal that you most want to work with.

The chosen goal then requires a specific structure to be successful. It must have a **What** and a **Why** component.

The 'What' is the answer to the question *'What specifically do I want to do about the goal?*

Then the 'Why' is the answer to the question *'why specifically is this valuable to me or what will I have that I don't have now when make this happen?'*

These responses then allow us to structure the goal in this particular way – *'I want to ..defined What...so that I..defined Why'*.

This is a well-structured and articulated goal.

Let's say that the answer to the greatest challenge is to 'beat my revenue targets this year' then to define that goal into a successful goal we need to *articulate* more fully.

The first question might be – 'by how much specifically do we want to beat our revenue target?' This then sets a *specific* outcome which is clear to the conscious mind.

Let's say it is 50% - we can either write down 50% or a specific financial value – but it must be specific. This is the WHAT part of the goal and would now be written:

'I want to exceed my revenue target by 50%...'

The next part is to ensure that we find the reason WHY this of value to us. This is the Toward motivation – or motive-in-action that drives our efforts and expectations.

Usually the Why is personal and highly specific.

For example in this goal it is easy to answer 'to make more money' but that is too general a reason. We need to ask 'why specifically is this important to me – what will I have that I don't have at the moment when I make this goal happen' – that is a powerful defining question.

From that might be *'so I can ensure my financial security'* or 'so that I can take the family on holiday this year' or so that 'I can create strong financial reserves' or 'secure a mortgage'. It is never just 'making more money' – it is always highly specific and personally relevant.

Now we write in the articulated form of *'I want to exceed my revenue targets by 50% so that I can create significant financial security'* – *that* is a well defined goal.

Then underneath this articulated goal we break it into initial manageable action steps. Make as complete a list as we can – come up with as many actions as possible - the more the better.

For example, if we were going to beat our revenue target by 50%, Step 1 might be to identify three new markets for networking for prospects, Step 2 revisit previous clients, Step 3 get more active on LinkedIn for referrals and so on.

There can be more than the initial five steps (in fact many more, and the simpler they are the better) but the first five or six serve to get us started on the process of making the desired outcome a range of mole hills rather than mountains.

Now, below these action steps write a brief description of the final thing that has to happen so that we know we have accomplished our goal.

In the case of this goal, it might be an image of us holding a bank statement with a very large cash reserve, or it might be a feeling of success in having beaten the targets or the sound of your family congratulating you on achieving the goal.

This is our *convincer*.

This is a clear signal to our conscious and unconscious minds that we have accomplished our target. In addition, it is also the creation of an internal visual representation that assists us in harnessing our internal energies towards the achievement of our outcome.

Then set the date. When will the goal be completed? As the great sales trainer Zig Ziglar once said 'goals are just dreams with a deadline'. If there is no specific date attached to the goal, all our careful planning is wasted.

Dates can be 3, 6 and 9 months away or even more depending on the size of the goal. What is most important is that we set a day, a month and the year – as this focuses the mind wonderfully on a specific deadline for completion.

The Action Plan
From this initial goal-setting exercise we might set two or three goals.

If so then we might want to create an Action Plan – something that allows us to choose selected actions from several goals so that we can focus on moving forward on all our goals at the same time - by focusing only on taking the actions that we assign to a given week.

Used weekly, the action plan continues the process of keeping our main goals in bite-size chunks which we can easily accomplish on a day-to-day, week-to-week basis. This then ensures that we get closer and closer to our successful outcomes.

The sheet is simple to create.

Take another piece of paper and write down - specifically and simply - up to five or six *accomplishable* things (selected from all of our chosen goals) that can be done in a given week that will bring you towards your outcome or outcomes.

Make sure that these things are in your ownership - that is that you are not depending on someone else to make it happen. Control what you control directly, *influence* through others what you do not control.

From the actions that we take weekly, new actions will then present themselves.

The dynamic that comes from taking action will present new challenges and opportunities that we need to address and so accomplish our desired goal.

To do so effectively, *prioritise* the new actions required on the action plan and complete them, and for even greater success not only *deadline the action plan* but *micro-deadline the actions* stating when in the week each action will itself be completed.

For this it can be excellent to have a colleague or a professional coach to be your performance partner, holding you accountable to yourself to deliver on the action plans and the goals.

Having someone who holds us accountable to ourselves, knowing that on a certain day at a certain time we have to sit down with someone and account for what we have or have not done is a powerful tool for keeping us on track and moving towards success.

Success will follow along with a greater sense of self-esteem and confidence in our abilities to create the world in our own unique way.

It's easy to fill anything at all on a blank canvas – completing a painting that has already been laid out requires more attention and produces more immediate and satisfying results.

High Trust Advisers know that their lives and careers move from 'mediocre to magnificent' and from 'success to significance', when we engage with effective goal setting.

Chapter 15: The 6 'C' Success Model

Now that we have an excellent sense of the power that goals can provide for us let's just put that in perspective and explain just how the clarity that goals give us can influence our behaviours.

As business advisers and account managers success is something we strive for everyday, so let me share with you a simple model for success every time.

I've called it 'The 6C Model' and it is something that I explain to my coaching clients when explaining how executive or business development coaching can deliver a real and tangible benefit to their practices and businesses.

The 6C's of the Model are: CONTEXT, CLARITY, CONTROL, CONFIDENCE, COMMUNICATION AND COMPETENCE.

1. CONTEXT: The first part of the model deals with *Context* or to be more specific, the *environment* in which we find ourselves working.

The environment in which we find ourselves working constantly changes and the pace of change may be such that we find ourselves *reacting* to the changes rather than being *proactive*.

We find ourselves working in a constant 'fire-fighting' mode just holding the line against the growing tide of work and the demands that our business seems to be heaping upon us.

The demands placed upon us are such that little time is available for active reflection and we are driven by external forces rather than by our own inner compass or agenda.

We tend to "Reflex" or simply unconsciously respond to stimuli, when we should "Reflect" or consciously choose the course of action that is most beneficial.

2. CLARITY: No matter how busy we are we can always benefit by taking some time out for *"enforced reflection"* – a time in our diary for space and time away from our normal environment and work pressures that allows us to get a greater sense of focus and purpose. But (and be honest) when did we do it last?

Lack of Clarity deprives us of the ability to focus and hence act effectively. It maximises stress. Focus is an essential part of performance.

As we've already seen our focus is composed of two areas - purpose and passion. Purpose is the "WHAT" it is we have to do - but passion is the "WHY".

By taking the time to understand clearly not just what we have to do, but the *reason and motivation* behind it we become charged with energy and act with purposeful and powerful intention.

3. CONTROL: With clarity accomplished, we should now find a greater sense of power over our environment. We are now in a position to *choose* our actions and activities.

All goals or objectives should be broken down into the smallest of actions – the many little things that make even the greatest of goals work.

The smaller the action the more likely it will be accomplished.

All goals and objectives (no matter how large) come down to the completion of the smallest of things.

My coaching clients are constantly surprised by how much they accomplish in a relatively short period of time during a coaching programme while still working under the usual pressures of the job.

The secret is in taking little actions, doing things that they directly control and that they can do when they 'leave a room'. This is important, an action is not something that be broken down into further actions, it is the smallest possible thing.

Each action accomplished then contributes to the dynamic of success that is building up, inexorably leading to the successful accomplishment of any goals.

4. CONFIDENCE: With control comes a greater sense of self-esteem, a belief in our ability to deliver.

Self-esteem increases when we have clear goals and the power to exercise them. Confidence is boosted by the successful achievement of 'quick hits' or small actions.

Success breeds success and with growing success comes more energy to do things, more self-belief and more self-confidence.

Every little action that we successfully complete boosts our self-esteem and subconsciously sets up the motivation to do more. We start aligning our focus with our motivation and then anything becomes possible.

5. COMMUNICATION: The first four "C's" lead unerringly to the fifth which is effective communication.

Good business comes down to the quality of the relationship and the quality of the communication between the prospect and the professional. This quality is further enhanced by the level of confidence and conviction in the message shown by the professional delivering the message.

Being confident in what we have to offer, in what we believe in, knowing where we are going (and why) and knowing that we ourselves control the steps that bring us there lends powerful conviction and congruence to our business message.

The High Trust Adviser by Seán Weafer

Personal confidence directly impacts on our body language, our tone of voice, our sense of inner certainty - key factors to being a powerfully convincing communicator.

During a recession it's good to remember that recession is not a crisis of money but a crisis in trust and confidence. In difficult markets and difficult times often people are looking for direction and they look to those who inspire confidence and certainty in their messages.

As a result, professional advisers, consultants and key account managers who understand and apply the emotional dynamics at work in being a High Trust Adviser have a wonderful opportunity to lead the business field.

The essence of good communication in business today can be explained by a simple idea – "**C.I.E.**".

Connect
Involve
Engage

So how do we "Connect, Involve and Engage" more effectively?

By learning techniques such as active questioning and listening, establishing rapport, reframing, networking, profiling people and defining their communications preferences and then adapting our personal style to suit them.

These are the tools of "CIE" and collaboration. Lastly, the final 'C' is:

6. COMPETENCE: Put all of the above together and we come up with top-level performance. The capacity to outlast, outperform and outsell all of our competitors.

To be able to provide the best of services or solutions in the most professional of manner to our clients and prospects, that is the mark of success.

If Context, Clarity, Control, Confidence and Communication are developed and strengthened then there is a corresponding increase in our Competence or performance and so …success!

In our next chapter I'll discuss some key strategies for managing our most valuable asset – time.

Chapter 16: Managing Your Professional Time

Busy professionals can be constantly time challenged. The question is ...are they being efficient or effective?

Efficient means that you are doing the job right. Effective means that are you doing the *right job*.

I often find that a huge amount of professional time is wasted by our focusing on the wrong things. Working with my many coaching clients they consistently raise the issue of 'time management' being a problem.

My mentor and friend, the great Dr. Denis Waitley once said that 'Time management is a fallacy – you can't manage time. One cannot make an hour longer than it is or bring yesterday back'.

He said that it is our focus that we should manage and not our time. Manage your focus and time moves with you.

Would it not be fair to say that as relationship managers, professional advisers and consultants (where time and expertise are often our only resources) we too often get absorbed into the business and lose our sense of what also matters in life?

As a result we may find ourselves wishing there were 24 hours in the working day. We may find that we are re-acting and fire-fighting rather than being pro-active and in control. Not enough time for the important things like self and family.

If you'd like to get more power over your personal organisation and make more time to sell or spend time doing the important things in life then here are a few ideas on how to get back on top on your time:

Schedule "Virtual" Meetings.
Ask yourself this question...who is your most important client?

If they wanted to meet with you, right now - you'd meet them, wouldn't you? You'd drop everything to be there for them wouldn't you?

But how about reflecting on the fact that YOU are your most important client?

How about planning a regular weekly 'client' meeting with yourself, your "virtual self", sitting opposite you at the table and wanting to know where things are and what you need to do to get the most out of things?

Create a time in the diary every week when you have that meeting. Create a written agenda for what you want to "discuss." And this is one meeting that NEVER gets de-prioritised or re-scheduled.

Every one of us can benefit from the ability to create some enforced reflective space. But unless we diarise it and treat it like an important client meeting, it never happens.

Without investing in ourselves, pretty soon we run out of the energy to invest in others – and in our business, that's crucial.

Delegate!

Every High Trust Adviser should be able to delegate, but few know how to manage it. So here are some suggestions;

First, make a list of what exactly you can delegate. Think about what each hour of "routine stuff" that you can hand to someone else can earn you if you are working on the "money stuff."

Second, make a list of the talents of your team members, associates, colleague or sales support.

What are their strengths? What are their career goals? How can you help them grow – provide a reward - by allocating a relevant project or task to them? Let them show you what they can do for you. Delegate to their strengths.

Third, involve them in the solution of how best to handle the matter.

Discuss with them what exactly you want and invite their views on how they can make it happen. It doesn't always have to be your way. That which we co-create, we own. The more they shape how they will handle it, the more likely they are to take ownership and responsibility for it.

Lastly, agree to check back with them at regular intervals, and then let them get on with it.

Make Personal Time.
Why do you do what you do? Taking time out for you is the best way to re-charge, and it is something we all fail to do.

Years from now it won't be the late nights at the office that we will fondly remember, but the moments and memories with family and friends that forge the life we want to reflect fondly on. Family and friends may respect what we do, but it's us they love and want with them, not our work.

Surveys have shown that the most successful of business people routinely plan the vacations they intend to take at the start of each year.

Knowing they are taking regular breaks helps them to stay motivated for a specific, intense period of time. Then they go get rested – and come back with even greater energy.

Even weekly personal time can be beneficial…..all it takes is a decision.

Try this experiment. Head home, two days a week, every week, for the next three weeks at 5pm – no later. Start as early as you like, but lead the traffic home two days a week and plan something with family and friends.

Manage Your Focus and Your Professional Boundaries.
It's tempting to chase all the business there is, to go from contract to contract, deal to deal, especially if you're focused on the money matters. It's tempting to say 'we can do it' to every request that comes from clients or even colleagues.

The problem is that we quickly find that we are being very busy but not every effective. Then we blame time management as the problem.

The real challenge is managing our focus, *what* we really should be doing and *why* we really should be doing it. It's a bit like business meetings. How many business meetings do you attend that really are a waste of time.

Try this filter for the future:

Must Do – Nice to Do – Deferrable/Delegate-able and see how you win back more time for the important things.

Learn to push back by saying 'No' elegantly. Say 'No for Now' – do not accept things simply because they are out in front of you. Push back a little.

Ask:

'Does this need to be done now?' OR

'I am busy right now but I could get to it tomorrow would that be OK?' OR

'X is the real expert in this area you really should reach out to them...'

Just because people ask doesn't mean we always have to take something on board.

The CIA Formula
Effectiveness comes down to levels of control. The CIA formula which I drafted to help clients cope with managing focus is a great little tool for self-awareness of the limits of our control.

Make a list of things that you need to get done. Then apply the following formula:

C = Control - Act on What You Own (First Level of Control)
Mark the things that you directly have authority for and can make happen without reference to anyone else. Do these first.

I = Influence - Reach Out to Others (Second Level of Control)
This is about leverage and is where your internal networks become important.

We don't control this and so can't just make it happen. We need *to reach out and influence someone else* who has the power to make sure that it comes to pass.

This is therefore any goal or task that requires that we can influence someone else and therefore takes a little longer and we have less control over the outcome.

A = Accept for Now (Third Level of Control)
Actually this is more of a level of self-control.

I see too many professionals beating themselves up over things that they do not control and cannot influence, so there's really nothing that can be done here.

Just becoming aware of that and focusing on what you can directly control or have others influence for you makes us far more effective and happier.

We need to leave what we have no control or influence over alone. Then in time it will either become a 'C' or an 'I' or just fade away because it was never important in the first place.

Remember while our work is important, both to ourselves and our clients, we work to live, not live to work.

Take just some of these five steps and watch your energy rise and realise something …your business productivity increases when you take adequate personal time to recharge...and you take back control.

In our next chapter I include some thoughts and strategies for those who lead today's High Trust Advisers™.

Chapter 17: Profiting in Challenging Times

In a 'boom economy' we are only required to take client orders – as confidence is strong and clients are queuing up to spend their budgets. *Transactional* business is the order of the day.

However we now know that it requires a special kind of business person to thrive in more challenging times - someone who can engage in *transformational* (or relationship-based) business.

So far in this book we have explored the critical skills required to help us thrive and survive by becoming a High Trust Adviser™ - a professional who understands the power and can apply the dynamics of emotional and social intelligence to business relationships.

In this chapter I want to share some thoughts about the kinds of things that practice partners, directors and account directors might want to consider so that they can help their teams continue to thrive in a more challenging market.

Feng Shui Our Client List.

Feng Shui is the Chinese art of moving and placing objects within a room or space, so that positive energies can flow and benefit the inhabitant of that space.

It can be used to create a highly relaxing environment or to attract health or even good luck to a room or building. To me, while I am sure that there are powerful and ancient principles at play, it often seems like it's an exercise in de-cluttering and minimising.

De-cluttering is a good thing to do. It frees up space (either physically or mentally) and allows the opportunity for new things to come and occupy that space. Therefore we should consider de-cluttering our client databases.

Over the years we have collected clients that are neither productive nor profitable. These clients act as a drain on our time and resources. The demand, they complain and they want everything for nothing.

Instead of holding onto these clients we should actively remove them from our databases or de-prioritise the communication or the degree of contact that we give them.

They can create opportunities for our account managers or fellow advisers to 'hide behind' and justify their poor performance. They serve as 'black holes' for productivity and profit. Get rid of them – aggressively. Give them a business opportunity elsewhere.

You want them out so that good clients can inhabit the space and benefit from the resources that these poor clients are currently draining.

Feng Shui Our Team.

Ditto for the team. We have people on the team that our good performers are carrying.

We have people who have been able to 'coast' because the market was up and people were ordering. They weren't 'hunters' and they are only average 'farmers'.

To continue to carry people who have neither the skills, the aptitude and (most importantly) the attitude or desire to perform, is demoralising for the rest of the team and stressful for the business leader(s).

This is a weight that will only get heavier as the months and the years progress. Act now. Be clinical. Quick, surgical cuts heal cleanly. It's possible that they may prove more successful in another role or another firm. If you procrastinate it will only make things work. Assess your people and make the choices. Do it now.

You can even provide a coaching programme to help them gain the skills to step up to the mark or plan an exit – making space for productive team members or partners.

Lock in Our Clients.

With good clients now becoming a target for other firms and competitors, we have to take stronger measures to lock in the client that we have. We have to ensure their loyalty and their continued custom.

The High Trust Adviser by Seán Weafer

Advisers working in business development and account management should be prioritising their clients, reviewing previous spend, assessing the current and future value of the client and creating events and offers that encourage the client to keep coming back.

They should be finding ways to expand their profile and their presence within these clients. They should have their existing contacts open doors to other departments and decision-makers.

We should be setting targets for them not just about the financial results, *but the quality and the value of the personal contacts that they make.*

How thoroughly are we reviewing client account plans or do we have them at all? How focused are our people on their accounts? Without bringing clarity as to where our clients are at, we cannot give the adviser or key account manager a sufficient sense of control over that client relationship.

Create events that add value for our clients. Instead of the usual social events, think about sponsoring or creating events that help them with *their* challenges.

Can we sponsor sales training for *their* sales teams, coaching for their senior executives, management days or conference speakers? (for more on this check out www.SeanWeafer.com)

A relatively small marketing investment on our behalf might mean a huge value for the client, something that they will appreciate and can ensure continued loyalty to us. In addition, we could 'insert' our own people within these events and create closer relationships with their key people.

Simple things can be done too, like handwritten personal notes or gifts of relevant books, sometimes the personal touch can establish close bonds that can be the difference between retaining or losing a quality relationship.

Review Our Contact Chain

As a managing partner or business development director we have responsibility for not just driving business development but ensuring its retention also.

A 'contact chain' is like an audit trail of all the people involved in the sales or servicing process of the business.

From our service people, to expert professionals, to accounts people, to the front-line, first-contact people such as the important receptionists or telemarketing – a small thing like the wrong tone of voice or a distracted manner with a client – can lose us business.

Everyone sells and we can't afford mistakes.

Everyone in the business that in any way affects the perceptions or the emotional response of a client, is responsible for retaining or losing that 'profit-centre'. Anyone that is 'client-facing' has some responsibility for either retaining or creating revenue.

As a leader of professional advisers our responsibility is to take this message to the board and ensure that our peers and heads of other departments get the message.

They must take responsibility for the quality and professionalism that their people project. There is no room for 'kingdom thinking' in this new market place. No one person stands alone when it comes to the continued success of the business. Everyone depends on one another.

The board (in consultation with the team - because this must be a co-creative and not an imposed message) must work on what is the company brand or the message that, as leaders, they can sell to their 'internal customers' – their staff members and colleagues.

A message that is so simple and effective that it can be actively owned and internalised by staff, who can then authentically project it to the customer - an internal PCR if you will. The 'Million Dollar Message' that every staff member can communicate to clients.

I changed garages recently. That may not seem like a big thing but in the auto industry this can be crucial. Customers tend to like to stay with the garage they buy their car from.

They have a connection. It should be easy to hold onto them. Customers can often be brand conscious about their car and want to belong.

Losing a client might have been OK when times are good – sure if we lose one or two does it matter? But it does now.

Not only did I move garages but I was prepared to significantly inconvenience myself and pay more for the service, because I knew this new garage was more expensive. Why would I do such a thing? It's not logical, it doesn't make sense.

Probably not – but it *feels* right. My emotions made my decision.

The receptionist was the reason.

On two occasions when I arrived at the garage for work that needed doing, I was left standing in front of her while she finished a phone call or a social conversation with a colleague. Not a hint of recognition. Not a mouthed apology or 'I'll be with you in a second sir'- nothing.

I rang another garage.

The receptionist was pleasant, she was briefed, she took me through a serious of short pertinent questions and then arranged a time for my car.

I rang back again to change the date, to be spoken to by a different receptionist. She was equally well briefed, efficient, courteous, professional and pleasant. I promised myself that if they smiled at me when I came through the door (I know - I have acceptance issues..!) they would get the business for life. They did.

Review and (if needed) upgrade your client contact chain.

Positively Imagine
As a successful leader of High Trust Advisers you become consciously or unconsciously a role model for those who report to you. Our every mood is monitored and responded to by our team.

A number of years ago I wrote in a blog on my website about my youngest son (he was only 6 years old then) telling me a joke.

He said to me: *'Dad, imagine you were put in a box, then they locked the box and then they covered it with chains and then they dumped the box in the sea – what would you do?'*

Well I scratched my head, thought hard for a while and when told him I had no idea what I'd do and he shouted: *'STOP IMAGINING!!'* and fell over with laughter at how stupid a Dad can be...

Profound really when you think about.

The High Trust Adviser by Seán Weafer

Most recessions are crises of confidence and trust, not a lack of money, that's a symptom.

It is something that happens when a perception is created or taken on board by media, investors, business people and consumers. It is imagined.

Yes, there are global factors but humans are creative creatures – at least the ones that don't put their head in the sand when things look a little rough and hope to wait it out.

Creating positive 'imaginings' in the minds of ourselves and our business development teams creates an attitude of 'can do', a willingness not to make excuses because of the market but to discover new ways to work in the market and thrive.

'Fire tempers steel' a friend once said to me. Well the fire is now. The question is - will it melt us or make us stronger?

Only we as High Trust Advisers can determine that but first we must begin to 'positively imagine'.

Only then, with the very fibre of our being, can we communicate to our people that even tough times are not one of adversity but one of opportunity.

About Seán Weafer

Seán is an international author, speaker and coach on r'evolutionary business and personal purpose (how to evolve people and profits through the power of relationships) working mainly with technology and financial services businesses.

Also known as 'The Rebel in a Business Suit', he brings a force of positive provocation to businesses for (as he says) 'successful businesses are built by people not limited by the ordinary'.

He is the creator of The High Trust Adviser coaching/training seminar series for relationships managers, sales professionals and business advisers.

This seminar series shows relationship managers, business advisers and owners...how to move beyond trust to connection...and get 'invited' to do business...using the latest in sales psychology to create a proven, low pressure, high permission business development process.

His corporate clients include Standard Chartered Private Bank, Oracle Software, British Telecom, Systagenix Wound Management, HSBC, Microsoft, Grant Thornton, BDO and RSM.

He is also founder and CEO of www.SalesDojo.com a global membership website for micro-medium businesses who want to learn 'black belt' selling techniques, psychology and technology via weekly video updates and access to an archive of video and MP3 'info bite' seminars to grow their businesses and sales success.

Since 1997 he has been a business development/executive coach (and coach trainer), speaker, author and information product designer in communications, networking, business development, coaching and mentoring - in the Far East, Middle East, Europe and the USA.

He also created the philosophy and path of personal r'evolution 'The Way of the Noble Soul' and is the author of the executive coaching primer 'The Business Coaching Revolution'.

He is a noted facilitator and event presenter and is a Fellow of the Professional Speaking Association in the UK and a past founder member and Honorary Vice President of the Association for Coaching.

The High Trust Adviser by Seán Weafer

"Bringing Sean into our business in BT was a great move and results were almost immediate. If you want your team to get motivated and drive improved results, then hire Sean!"

Peter Russell, Head of NI Public Sector and Major Accounts, British Telecom

"I have worked with Sean on coaching and management development programs. I have engaged him for projects in Ireland, UK and the Middle East. Sean has consistently delivered outstanding results from the individuals and teams he has worked with. His dynamic, creative approach has been hugely popular and typically I have line managers and executives delighted with the results achieved. Sean understands business and knows how to help individuals, teams and organisations achieve their goals. I am delighted to recommend Sean and the services he provides"

Gerry Cleary, Senior HR Director at Websense International.

Contact Seán Weafer

Web: www.SeanWeafer.com

LinkedIn: http://ie.linkedin.com/in/SeanWeafer

Twitter: http://twitter.com/SeanWeafer

E-mail   Sean@SeanWeafer.com

You can take this online coaching programme for creating compelling client relationships at www.HighTrustAdviser.com

Or avail of some great free offers and the very best weekly 'video bytes' on selling and related matters by joining our sales mastery global community at www.SalesDojo.com

Made in the USA
Charleston, SC
26 January 2014